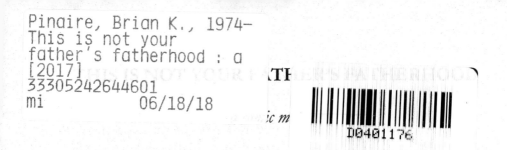

Brian K. Pinaire

MOONSHOT BOOKS

Portland, Oregon

PRAISE FOR *This Is Not Your Father's Fatherhood*

Brian K. Pinaire's *This Is Not Your Father's Fatherhood* stares down every myth about fatherhood—those good and bad—while providing enough laughter to prevent those of us who are fathers, and who ought to know better, from counting all our faults. This is a moving, compelling read and a reminder that parenting is a two-way street. Ours just leads to weirder neighborhoods.

-Saladin Ambar, Lehigh University

This Is Not Your Father's Fatherhood is a brilliant, funny, and incredibly well-written series of essays about coming of age while coming to grips with the new, wondrous, taxing, and bewildering realities of a previously simple, straightforward life. Pinaire's engaging prose, his integration of pop culture from multiple realms—movies, books, TV, music—and his "Seinfeld-esque" tone had me laughing out loud. This book's mixture of humor, insight, gravitas, and sentiment will leave you loving its characters.

-Milton Heumann, Rutgers University

Pinaire's colorful tale is brutally honest, gut-buster funny, and yet warmhearted and nostalgic. Save the money you'll pay a therapist to get over the guilt of fatherhood. Just buy this book and laugh your way to an acceptance of the fact that you, too, may have been the "World's Best Dad."

-Richard Matthews, Lehigh University

Reading Brian K. Pinaire's book is like hanging out with the coolest dad on the playground. He can make you laugh about the naiveté of your birth plan, make you see Dora and Diego in a whole new way, and make a mesmerizing story out of wearing a BabyBjörn. And along the way, he can make you feel so, so good about spending your adulthood with your kids. Pinaire's boys are clearly lucky to have him as a dad, and the rest of us are lucky to have him as a storyteller.

-Susan McWilliams, Pomona College

ALSO BY BRIAN K. PINAIRE

The Constitution of Electoral Speech Law

This is a comic memoir. The events, experiences, and encounters de-scribed within are all real and really happened, although some accounts have been enlivened by hyperbole. Names, essences, and locations have been obscured to protect both innocent and guilty parties.

Moonshot Books is based in Portland, Oregon. Its mission is to think big, take chances, resist convention, tell stories that need to be heard, and produce books for the sake of books.

www.brianpinaire.com

www.moonshotbooks.com

www.thisisnotyourfathersfatherhood.com

Pinaire, Brian K., 1974–
    This is not your father's fatherhood : a comic memoir / Brian K. Pinaire
    ISBN 978-0-692-80299-1
    1. Humor. 2. Biography & Autobiography.

Author photograph by Jan Pinaire

Internal photographs by Brian K. Pinaire

ABOUT THE AUTHOR

Brian K. Pinaire is the author of *The Constitution of Electoral Speech Law* and dozens of articles in both commercial outlets and academic journals. He holds a BA in politics from Whitman College and a PhD in political science from Rutgers University.

Pinaire was formerly a tenured professor of political science at Lehigh University, where he received multiple awards for teaching and research. Since retiring from academia, he has worked as a full-time writer, researcher, and editor.

A native of Omaha, Nebraska, Pinaire currently resides in Portland, Oregon, with his wife, Emily, and their two sons, Lucas and Wills. He took a semester-long paternity leave (twice) and found himself forever changed by changing diapers. Being a father is the hardest thing he's ever done—but also the best.

For my father

CONTENTS

INTRODUCTION

> The birth of his son opened Theobald's eyes to a good deal which he had but faintly realised hitherto. He had no idea how great a nuisance a baby was.
>
> -Samuel Butler

CARING FOR THINGS WAS NEVER MY THING. Freedom was my thing. Detachment was also my thing—as well as distance, especially emotional distance, selfishness, unavailability, and a lack of empathy. So, too, was it my thing to be raspy, aloof, jaded, judgmental, exceedingly impatient, and sometimes kind of a jerk.

Since having kids, I've fallen away from many (or at least some) of those things, but I still have great memories of them. They were so good about letting me sleep late, swear with impunity, watch *SportsCenter* at one *and* two o'clock in the morning (just to see if anything new had happened), drink too much, smoke, work around the clock, leave dishes piled up, pack only one small bag for a trip, scowl at babies on airplanes, ignore feelings, frustrate attempts at closeness, practice professional-grade introversion, and generally move through life without any responsibilities other than those that satisfied my immediate interests.

Back in those days, I was accustomed to taking care of myself and nothing more—which was how I liked it. It was an extension of my life as an only child, where I relished independence, where I was alone much of the time, where I never volunteered as a youth coach or camp counselor, where I had no desire to play "family" with my various toy action figures, and where I was on my way to becoming the grumpy old man on the block who chases away kids with a rolled-up newspaper whenever they walk across his lawn.

Little ones were never what I saw myself working toward and never what I would have considered my greatest accomplishment in life. If I contemplated children at all, they were mere abstractions: possibly in my future but no more so than any other potential occurrences of adulthood, like a retirement account or a Costco membership. The only way kids could or would fit into the portrait of my life was if they didn't crowd out more important things like work, wealth, maybe a wife, and more work.

It's funny how foolish you are until you become wise.

You think you know it all, but you really know nothing. You think you have yourself sized up, but you are way off the mark. Until you actually have children, you can't apprehend the feelings that attend to them—feelings you may not have known even existed. And you certainly can't imagine going from not caring much at all to feeling a degree of care so profound it supplants all other cares in the world.

But this is exactly what happened to me. And it's also exactly why I resisted it for so long—because such a connection made me feel vulnerable, such devotion exposed me too much, and such dedication stripped me of control. You see, those with my personality disorder believe that if you stack nothing up, nothing can fall down. Opening yourself up to love and potential loss, and to attachment and perhaps separation, takes courage—courage I could not muster.

Until I could.

Fatherhood would not have seemed to be a good match for a man like me—and it wasn't.

Until it was.

I could never have realized this back when I knew so much of nothing at all, but life refused my projections and denied my initial forecast. Which is what makes this story worth reading and, for those fortunate enough to do so, worth replicating.

When you end up somewhere by default not design, when you are lost and won't ask for directions, when you used to sleep at a desk but eventually stumbled over to a rocking chair, and when you've walked the road to enlightenment while stepping on LEGOs the entire way, you wonder what the hell just happened. It gives you pause.

You pinch yourself. Or you punch yourself. Or you take a few shots. Or you write a book. Or you do all of the above.

THE FUNNY THING IS, I almost missed the chance that made all the difference. It was fall 2004, and my wife, Emily, was pregnant with our first child, Lucas. We were finally starting to think seriously about childcare, trying to figure out how we could manage a newborn while maintaining two careers in their early stages.

At the time, I was an assistant professor at a university in the northeast, and Emily was in medical school about three hours away. I lived in one city; she lived in another. We drove a lot. It was hard—or at least it seemed hard by the standards of life before children.

Because I was preoccupied teaching new classes, trying to publish as much as possible, handling service commitments, and practicing the usual politics of research universities, Emily was the one who devised our plan to start a family. For her part of this planning, she talked with other women in her program who'd had children and figured out a way to front-load her electives so she would be able to take several weeks of maternity leave at the end of her final year. And for my part of this planning, I . . . well, I didn't really have a part, actually. Or maybe I did, but I just wasn't paying any attention to it.

I'm sure I didn't intend to take any time away from work. I would never have planned on that. That's not because I thought Lucas would be Emily's responsibility; it's more that I just wasn't thinking about the baby at all. Our new addition wasn't right in front of me, and it's hard to give serious consideration to something like paternity leave when you have yet to register the notion of paternity itself.

Neither of us realized just how disruptive it would be to start a family at this time, especially the ways our respective professional pursuits would be affected. I guess we thought we would just muddle through as people do, putting Lucas in daycare as soon as possible and doing whatever the hell else parents do when they're juggling two careers and a small child. In hindsight, it was a remarkably unplanned plan—and one probably destined to fail.

Until one day in January 2005, when I actually read one of the flyers that had been stuffed into my academic department mailbox. Usually, I ignored these things, since most of them were from some office on campus that no one had heard of, but this one caught my attention. Coming from Human Resources, it explained an option that allowed eligible faculty and staff members to take up to twelve weeks of family leave to care for a child in the first year of life: twelve weeks of family leave *with* full pay and benefits.[*]

That sounds like an amazing opportunity, doesn't it?

This was not just a Family and Medical Leave Act (FMLA) leave (i.e., time away from work that federal law requires certain employers to make available, albeit without compensation); this was a funded leave. This was a leave where I would get a check every month without having to write lectures, grade papers, or listen to other professors blather on at meetings. This was a leave where all I needed to do was whatever you do with a baby every day for three months.

Most normal people would have jumped at this deal.

But not me.

At least not right away.

If that seems dumb to you, I agree. It was. Not only was this a chance to bond with our first child, but Emily was about to begin a notoriously competitive medical residency with a grueling schedule and

---

[*] This option might be hard to fathom (unless you are European), but more American employers have started subsidizing such policies to help employees realize a better work-life balance. Universities, in particular, do this kind of thing a lot, because they fancy themselves progressive institutions, if there is such a thing, but also because they are competing with one another for faculty, especially female faculty, for whom such allowances can make the difference in terms of recruitment and retention.

generally inflexible structure. Those residents in her program who were married didn't always stay married, and those who had children almost always had a stay-at-home spouse, a nanny, or some other person helping out. In fact, it's almost impossible to do this combination of things any other way. A right-thinking person would have realized that our plan would never work, that something had to give.

Looking back, I can recognize what we should have seen; but in the moment, I wasn't trying very hard to look for it. I had worked for many years to earn a PhD, was lucky to have a tenure-track position at a great institution, and was totally fixed on getting promoted. I wasn't thinking about taking one for the team, slowing down and smelling the roses, or bonding with anything other than my laptop.

No matter how good the family-leave deal was, I wasn't interested. It just wasn't for me. Workaholics want to be in the corner office as much as alcoholics want to be in the corner bar.

That sounds bad, but wait—it gets worse. I did eventually decide to take a family leave, but I did so for all the wrong reasons. The more my woefully ignorant, impossibly naïve, and totally warped mind mulled it over, the more I started to think: *Hmmm, if I don't have to teach classes, just imagine how much writing I could get done!*

Yes, you read that correctly: I decided to take a leave from work so I could do less of one kind of work and more of another.

I figured I would fumble around with "baby stuff" for an hour or so in the morning, perhaps reading Lucas a book or letting him look out the window, after which he would nap for maybe six or eight hours and then sit quietly in the high chair, feed himself, and listen intently as I read him my best paragraphs of the day. It seemed like an easy opportunity to be more productive while also being a "parent," whatever that meant.

What a completely stupid notion that was.

On the one hand, even while I was on leave, I still had official duties that couldn't wait—service commitments, letters of recommendation to write, and emails to respond to from people who apparently couldn't wait twelve minutes for an answer, let alone twelve weeks. And on the other hand, to be "off" while caring for a young child is simply to be "on" in a different way. Family leave doesn't give you more time to work, it just gives you more work.

And harder work, honestly, which I realized on my first official day of leave in fall 2005, as a part of me—a large part of me, actually—regretted this decision. I yearned to be *at* work, not away from it. I wanted to be in my office and doing my job, not in my living room and feeling tired, frustrated, and totally inept with a six-month-old baby.

By the end of that first day, I had already had enough—and I still had eleven weeks and six days to go. With every passing week, however, I became a more competent, capable, and confident caregiver, finding that three months of hands-on, self-directed training was just what I needed for innate resistance and inherited responsibilities to reconcile their differences.

This experience was also essential preparation for the next several years, because even when I went back to a normal work routine, I was still the parent responsible for most of the childcare. Emily's residency, which was followed by a yearlong fellowship in her area of specialty, and then an even more demanding schedule as a clinical assistant professor and attending physician, required her to spend long hours at the hospital. This is typical for medical professionals, and I probably should have seen it coming, but I had been too focused on my own career to anticipate the collateral effects of her profession.

Emily would leave stores of breast milk and check on us all the time, but she was generally on her way to work before dawn and not home until seven o'clock at night, except for overnight shifts when she wasn't home at all. By contrast, while I had to be on campus to teach a few days per week, I could write, grade, and prepare for class from home. This arrangement had me running point on childcare every morning, nearly every evening, many weekends, and most days when

Lucas was sick, while also attending events at the daycare or preschool, pretending to cook, shopping for the groceries, and managing most of the other tasks that keep a household running.

Every family has its own version of this predicament, its own micro-economy and division of labor. Perfectly equal distributions of domestic responsibility only exist in theory, so it's almost necessarily the case that *someone*—one or the other spouse or partner in a two-person situation—will bear more of the burden with respect to family affairs. Someone needs to make sure the trains run on time. Someone needs to move the bodies around. Someone needs to be here for this and take care of that. And by convention—as well as economic forces, tradition, mom-guilt, lazy dads, and other influences—that "someone" is usually a mother.

But not in our case. And not in the case of an increasing number of households in the United States. Indeed, as research on Generation X and millennial men indicates, not only are today's dads more involved in domestic affairs than their own fathers were, they generally *want* this greater involvement.

It's true that fathers may not feel as motivated (read: pressured) to volunteer at their kids' schools, and may not be as inclined to attend PTA meetings, fret over nutrition, engage in playground politics, read articles on parenting blogs, or do the innumerable other things mothers do, or the things mothers think they should do, but that doesn't mean dads are tuned out. And it definitely doesn't mean they can't handle being in charge. It just means they do things in a different way.

Which is okay—good, even.

A dad isn't just a mom with facial hair. He's a dad. He's his own thing. He doesn't have to follow written instructions for the kids; he can write his own instructions.

Or maybe he doesn't even need instructions. Maybe he can just wing it. Maybe he learns best by trial and error. And maybe he'll find himself taking pride in something he wanted nothing to do with before, perhaps even champing at the bit to do things better the next time—just as I was in fall 2008, when I took another semester of family leave, this time with our second child, Wills.

By that point, I had no expectation of getting work done with an infant in my lap. I merely hoped to achieve the same deep, meaningful connection with Wills that I had developed with Lucas. It's not that I cared about work any less—to the contrary, I was up for tenure that year—it's more that, having been a primary caregiver, I finally started to recognize obligations beyond myself. Because I had to, initially; but because I *wanted* to, eventually.

It took some time, for sure, but big ships turn slowly.

Cast of Characters

NAMES	ROLES	QUALITIES	AGE
Lucas	Son, older brother	Sensitive, shy, cerebral, well-behaved, courteous, laughs at cartoons from *The New Yorker*	b. 2005
Wills	Son, younger brother	Brash, confident, charismatic, extroverted, reckless, laughs at farts	b. 2008
Emily	Wife, mother, physician	Sweet, intelligent, beautiful, devoted, optimistic, inspiring	b. mid-1970s
Brian	Husband, father, professor/writer	Salty, sarcastic, difficult, jaded, pragmatic, realistic	b. mid-1970s

ADOPTING A ROLE NEVER ENVISIONED, screwing up in all sorts of ways, benefiting from time and experience to come up to speed, and finding things out about myself along the way helped me to become a better father, husband, and man.

But not without many, many struggles along the way.

Many, many struggles.

Struggles every day.

Even now. Even still.

Like *today*, in fact—on whatever day you're reading this.

While books on parenting and family life often take a prescriptive tone, lapse into navel-gazing, or proffer saccharine (and usually self-serving) depictions of domestic affairs, you won't get that here. To the contrary, the pages below indicate a complete lack of awareness, intuition, initiative, ability, and even interest from the outset—with many of those same failings carried on to this day.

I didn't know what I was doing when I first became a father, and I still don't in many respects—which is why this work amounts to neither a dad-improvement manual nor a how-to book in any way, shape, or form. I suppose it could be seen as a how-*not*-to book in some sense—and, certainly, the reader is welcome to draw that conclusion—but that would still be guidance, as it were, only by implication.

Instead, what I have offered is a collection of carefully integrated essays that—through anecdotes, observations, insights, research, and humor—strive to make sense of modern fatherhood by making fun of it. The result is an alternately sarcastic and sentimental attempt to explore those things a father thinks but isn't supposed to say; to examine what he feels but rarely admits; and to consider what he learns but may still (and perhaps always) struggle to understand.

Such as, for example, why it is that, on a certain Sunday in June every year, his children give him a card, tie, letter opener, or coffee mug emblazoned with words declaring him WORLD'S BEST DAD!

Even when he clearly isn't.

And even when he actually sucks some of the time.

Or maybe a lot of the time.

Your average dad realizes (or should realize) the kids' assessment isn't literally true—that he would never win an actual competition for "best" father on the planet—but he also realizes (or comes to realize) that a swig of well-intended hyperbole takes the edge off hard truths.

Even if most of his time is devoted to being a murderous dictator or hedge-fund manager, a father can still be the "best" dad in the limited, bounded, and fantastically small world of those children in his lap—

youngsters who, thankfully, don't know any better, bless their little hearts.

Of course, accepting a ranking not technically warranted requires some cognitive dissonance on dad's part, but it's no different from what he does every weekend when he suspends disbelief, smiles at the camera, waves a foam index finger, and chants "We're number one!" for a team, squad, or unit that was eliminated from contention before the season even began.

If you are able to adopt this mindset and act in this manner—that is, if you can process how two plus two sometimes equals five, even if it doesn't—this book is for you.

If you publicly encourage green vegetable consumption with the passion of Popeye the Sailorman, while still privately gorging on tater tots, this book is for you.

If you sit down at the restaurant and immediately place the beer list inside the children's menu, so it seems like you are attending to the needs of the youngsters first, this book is for you.

If you are a man (or were at some point) who went into battle wearing a BabyBjörn, enduring snickers from other men while enjoying looks from women who would never have given you the time of day before you had a small human being strapped to your chest, this book is for you.

If you are a father who wondered how in the world you could "help" in the delivery room when men really don't have anything to do in there, or who reads to your kids at night but also makes up subplots along the way for your own amusement, or who adjusts the clocks to make bedtime come a few hours sooner, or who throws little ones into the air and usually catches them, or who is willing to take junior to the latest children's movie because it presents a great opportunity for a nap, this book is for you.

If you are a mother who would like a peek into the Dad Mind, this book is also for you. You'll get it.

If you are a childless woman or man who is perhaps contemplating a family someday, this book may or may not be for you. You would laugh; yet you might also laugh it off. You could think I'm kidding, which I am in many places, but which I'm not in others.

If you are a guy (or gal) who thinks that raising children is "women's work," this book is almost certainly not for you. You would just shake your head, grumble, and think: *What a fool.*

But that's fine. It's mutual.

I actually feel bad for you. You're missing out. Try suspending disbelief, smiling at the camera, waving a foam index finger, and chanting "World's Best Dad!" The game is about to start.

FATHER'S DAY

Resolved by the Senate and House of Representatives of the United States of America in Congress assembled, That the third Sunday in June of each year is hereby designated as "Father's Day."

-Public Law 92-278

FATHER'S DAY IS A HOLIDAY you can avoid if you are so inclined. Unlike Halloween, where the kids knock on your door despite the fact that you have your lights off; or Christmas, which starts finding you in September as the stores begin their pre-pre-holiday specials; or your birthday, when people never fail to remind you that you are one year closer to death, you don't have to be a part of Father's Day. You can steer clear of that Sunday celebration in June every year by simply not being anyone's father.

You may still have some obligations on that day, of course, perhaps showing some love to the poor man who has had to call you his son all these years, but if you are not interested in receiving that card, tie, letter opener, or coffee mug, that's your prerogative. It's within your control. Don't become a dad. Just continue with all those techniques of avoidance you learned when you were younger—back when society invested considerable resources into discouraging you from prematurely becoming a parent. When you were taught all about "protection" for yourself and the world. When it was obvious you were not "ready." And when everyone urged you to please, please, please not make a "mistake."

A mistake. That's what they called it.

It's an interesting word, actually, especially in this context, because as we learn but don't always want to admit, mistakes of youth can also be mistakes of adulthood. What was not right for a boy in his teenage years might also not be right for a man in his twenties, thirties, or forties. Or beyond. Or ever, in fact. Even when he's much older, that is, it could still—could always—be the case that fatherhood simply isn't a good fit for a man. There are plenty of perfectly happy guys with no kids and plenty of totally miserable guys with lots of kids.

You won't find this message printed in a Hallmark card, but what if it's the case that some men just shouldn't have anything to do with reproduction? What if they shouldn't go—or shouldn't have gone—that direction in life? What if they're entirely self-absorbed, insufferable assholes, too fearful of commitment, hopelessly incapable of affection, or just ramblin' men inclined to ramble off to other parts as soon as the whole fatherhood thing gets to be too much?

The children of such men could certainly still turn out fine, perhaps winning Olympic gold medals, becoming decorated soldiers, or curing cancer. But couldn't those youngsters also grow up to become the next Son of Sam, Adolf Hitler, Bernie Madoff, or Vanilla Ice? Those guys all had dads, didn't they? And can't we assume their fathers did something (or didn't do something) to make them that way?

You see? These are the stakes.

SOME MEN ARE DISCOURAGED from breeding any future versions of themselves as early as elementary school, when observers (and victims) of their terroristic tendencies on the playground make repeated calls to law enforcement agencies. But most guys get the hard press against hasty procreation in middle school. Or perhaps high school.

This is the age when a boy pretending to be a man learns that a mistake could delay or even destroy his plans to play in the NFL, become president, tour the world on a surfboard, or own a lawnmower shop. It's when he hears a lot about exercising discretion and good judgment—neither of which is a characteristic typically associated with adolescent males. And it's when he sits through a Sexual Education (Sex Ed) or similar sort of class that often toes an imprecise line between awareness and advocacy, cautiously casting "sexy" topics in only the most clinical terms.

Students today probably already know everything (or a version of everything) about sex before they even take a Sex Ed course, likely gleaning that "everything" (or version of "everything") from the Internet. They might even be educating themselves with considerable frequency as they stare at images on their smart phones that my generation could only see late at night on Cinemax. Back then, we weren't able to sit down at a computer (or pull one from our pocket) and search for answers to our burning questions.

One could always look to the familiar standbys of books, siblings, friends, or parents, but those were hit-or-miss options—and mostly just misses, actually. The books with really good pictures were always checked out or "lost"; siblings would just feed you bullshit so you would sound stupid in the locker room; friends never knew any more than you did; and no one asked their parents anything.

Enjoying society's indirect blessing by way of tax dollars and elected board members, *school* was the last, best option for teaching students about sex. Typically, this meant putting a grown woman in the awkward position of standing before a classroom of boys pretending to be men and then asking her to educate them on the nuances of the vagina.

In theory, this might sound like a nice thing for a boy pretending to be a man: to have a real, live woman telling him all about the sex part he's so interested in yet has no understanding of whatsoever.

But it wasn't. It wasn't a nice thing at all, in fact.

On the one hand, *vagina* is really *not* a good word. It's a perfectly good sex part, for sure; but as a word, it elicits looks from adolescent males that range from mild queasiness to outright angst. And on the other hand, dialogue with not-too-bright boys pretending to be men is nearly always discouraged by excessively dispassionate depictions of otherwise fascinating concepts.

Such a rendition virtually guarantees those glazed looks familiar to anyone who's ever been a teacher, suggesting a degree of detachment that could cause serious problems for society down the line. Students can't connect the dots if they won't pick up the pencil. And thus, a shrewd instructor—detecting this sort of queasiness, angst, apprehension, and weirdness—finds other ways to engage the clientele.

As it was in our case, this meant having an anonymous-question box outside the classroom. This method allowed education and embarrassment to meet in the middle by giving students the chance to pose queries without attribution or association. Tactics for ensuring anonymity varied, but most kids tried to disguise their handwriting by using the cursive script they learned in third grade but had not used since. Or they glued together cutout letters like the kind kidnappers use on ransom notes. Or they pulled the "asking-for-a-friend" move that people use when they are obviously asking for themselves.

All of this, just to be in position to set forth some of those burning questions, such as: "Does the drug store really keep dental dams in the toothbrush aisle?"; "Is it true that a woman's clitoris is in the small of her back?"; "Has anyone else got white bumps on their dong? (Asking for a friend.)"; "The textbook is unclear. Does a girl have two or three holes down there?"; and "Would you say a blow job is more like rounding second base but getting picked off at third, or more like touching all the bases but still not actually scoring a run?"

Answers varied according to the apparent authenticity of the question. Our teacher would respond to some queries in writing, posting her comments on the bulletin board, often with page references to the textbook we never read. She would ignore especially puerile submissions stuffed into the box by especially puerile individuals who happened to sit in the back-left corner of the room. And she used selected offerings, or iterations of selected offerings, to initiate the day's discussion, particularly when those offerings could be utilized to urge us to please, please, please not get—or get anyone—pregnant.

"Class," our war-weary teacher asked one day, holding one of those selected offerings in her hand, "do any of you know someone who has chosen to have sexual intercourse?" She always liked to put it that way, as if sex were simply a matter of "choice." As if it were ever that easy. As if it were just like choosing to see a movie or not. Every boy pretending to be a man in the room had "chosen" to have sex. The problem was finding a girl willing to honor that choice.

"You know, it only takes one time to get pregnant," she continued, taking the smirks on our faces as collective assent. "And it *can* be the first time," she added, because for some reason stupid teenagers think otherwise.

More smirks, more collective assent.

"So," she carried on, steeled in the pragmatism of secondary education, "if you *do* choose to become sexually active, what are some prophylactic measures you might take?"

We all knew what she was getting at here (I think), but phrasing questions with vocabulary terms no young person actually uses pretty much ensures several moments of absolute silence, followed by the sound of crickets willing to chirp till the end of time, if necessary. When faced with a question anchored by an intimidating four-syllable word like *prophylactic*, the leaders of tomorrow quietly flip to the glossary and hope someone else will say something.

Or that the bell will ring soon.

"You don't need to look up that word," our teacher rushed in to say this particular morning, recovering the moment. "What I mean is, what are some ways you can prevent pregnancy?"

Cue a few more moments of absolute silence and then a couple more crickets. *Pregnancy* has a mere three syllables, but still. You'd be surprised.

No matter, though. As most servants to the learning process are inclined to do, our teacher would go ahead and answer this question herself. When the stakes are this high, education cannot be entrusted to the students. The girls in the class needed good, solid information on "the pill," an option sufficient for most of them, although we also learned of other methods that were recommended for those young ladies with both aggressive weekend agendas and a demonstrated difficulty with daily rituals. (Not surprisingly, this required us to direct anticipatory glances around the room, suggesting which fair maidens might be in need of these more drastic measures.)

Then, turning toward the boys pretending to be men in the class, our teacher underscored a young male's role in the please, please, please do not get—or get anyone—pregnant-project, wondering of us, "Gentlemen," even though that salutation always seemed like a stretch, "what are some prophylactic measures *you* might take?"

Absolute silence.

Chirp. Chirp. Chirp.

"Sorry," she retracted, showing a deft ability to descend to the lowest common denominator for the good of the cause, "what I mean is, how can *you* prevent pregnancy?"

Clearly, every boy pretending to be a man had something to say about this, since we all had circle imprints on the outside of our wallets. But we still couldn't give her the answer she wanted.

To raise your hand and say "Condoms" would make you sound like a dork. And to take out your wallet and show her your circle imprint would make you look like a dork. The only thing we could do was offer a few more smirks signifying collective assent, facial expressions that indicated we knew, or mostly knew, what she wanted us to know. And what society needed us to know.

Still, just to be sure we embraced the message and internalized its importance, these in-class conversations were supplemented with a simulation-style assignment that required us to carry an egg everywhere we went for two weeks. Two very long weeks. Two hellishly long weeks, in fact.

We knew this exercise was a fixture of the course, but we still had to laugh when our teacher described it. It seemed so silly. Was this what happened when schools gave up on education—they just started handing out things from the dairy aisle? What could anyone possibly learn from two weeks of holding, transporting, and talking to the main ingredient of a breakfast sandwich?

We were still laughing, albeit not as much, when our teacher returned from the fridge in the Teachers' Lounge and started passing out our babies, insisting that we name them, take them with us everywhere, never let them out of our sight, and not even think of trying to cover up an infanticide by buying a dozen replacement youngsters at the grocery store. By then, no one was laughing. Because this sucked. (You could even say it sucked eggs if you had no standards for a joke.)

Keeping Humpty Dumpty from falling off his wall took our focus off more important high school activities, like standing in a circle by our lockers and looking at other people standing in a circle by their lockers. Two weeks isn't much time in the real terms of parenthood, but it's an eternity for a teenager. Fortunes can change by the minute at this age. Girls can bat eyes at you in the morning but black out your name on their notebook covers by dismissal. You can be ushered into the top clique but then booted from it within the same homeroom period. You can have seventeen new zits by lunch. And so on.

Nothing can truly capture the experience of caring for a child, except perhaps tending to an aging parent who needs help going to the bathroom, who chews on everything, who cries for no good reason, and who picks fights with a sibling just because that person happens to be alive, but carrying the egg gave us at least an approximation of the job. Especially with regard to its burdens. And its constancy. And the degree of attention required to actually be responsible for something other than yourself all the time.

Which is good, it seems. We *want* boys pretending to be men thinking this way during a time in their lives when they aren't thinking much at all: at a defining moment in their Y-chromosome existence when they have hopefully agreed to please, please, please not get anyone pregnant and when they are already overwhelmed enough as it is just bagging groceries, taking out the trash, and studying for a math test.

When, in other words, they just aren't "ready" for fatherhood—when it would be a "mistake."

IN MOST OF LIFE'S ARENAS, you must officially demonstrate ability and *earn* increments of authority. If you do your job well and show you can handle it, you get more responsibility. Existing metrics move you along, external validation opens doors of opportunity, and calculated leaps of faith put you in positions of trust. If you can avoid the temptations of turkey bowling in the aisles, for example, you might be allowed to manage the night shift at the grocery store. And if you prove you can control yourself around sugary delights, you could get promoted to the rank of assistant to the regional manager at Donut Delirium.

For those looking to assume roles or positions of consequence, some pre-planning is the norm, some prior expression of intention is required, and some exhibition of ability (or at least capacity) is generally expected. Take a look next time you are sitting in the swivel chair, fearing for your life in the backseat, or discussing the price of a coffin, and you will notice that barbers, taxicab drivers, and funeral directors, as but a few examples, typically must be either licensed or certified. As a society, we tend to require this sort of thing for professionals.

In the same regard, if you want to build a deck in your backyard, you usually need a permit. If you want to operate a food truck, you will likely require inspections. And if you want to buy a used car from Ed's Big Lot, you may need a background check to authorize the financing.

But what is required to become a father? Who presses you for a statement of purpose, credentials, references, or a blueprint when you want to make a person? We insist on those kinds of things when you want to *adopt* a person, for sure, but not when you want to create one.

Even more, at the Big Lot, Ed himself often emerges at the end of the deal and reminds you to change the oil. Or he cautions you against leaning too hard on the left side of the vehicle on days when it rains. Yet does anyone provide an owner's manual or customized pro tips when you decide to become a dad? No, of course not—which is a fact that is both obvious and curious at the same time.

Where else but in the world of parenting, and perhaps in the realm of fatherhood in particular, do we accept not knowing what to do, not knowing how to do it, and not being all that sure you really even *want* to do it as sufficient grounds for doing something? What other domain so regularly allows people to be in charge when they have no idea what's going on?

Don't say "politics." That's too easy.

Seriously, if a guy drew up a business plan that said, "I know I'm kind of a shithead, but I want to borrow some money so I can go out and make some little shitheads," would he get any investors? I mean, beyond a few other shitheads?

Probably not.

Why?

Because his business plan seems like a bad bet?

Probably.

And yet, if this same guy showed up at the bar one night and announced, "Me and the missus are having a kid—and we're naming him *Baby*," would he get a few rounds on the house?

Probably.

Why?

Because it's up to him and the missus if they want to have a kid—and if they want that kid to have a name like *Baby*?

Probably.

How can this be?

Before, when this guy was just a boy pretending to be a man, social structures worked their darnedest to emphasize that he was not ready. But then he turned into a man (still pretending to be a man) and . . . what? What changed, other than the number of candles on his birthday cake? What justified his departure from the "not ready" category?

Was it just the passage of time?

Being socially promoted to the status of "grown-up" can imply some greater capacity, increased financial security, slightly more stability, and so on, which can all help, but is that enough? Adulthood is a proxy for maturity in many ways, but does it signify the right *mentality*?

That's the funny thing about fatherhood. After all those years of organized deterrence, a guy suddenly finds that society has effectively reversed course; that, while previously denying his readiness, it is now prepared to give him the benefit of the doubt.

Because it has to, essentially. This *is* a free country, after all.

Anyhow, if you think about it, what does "ready" even mean?

Can you ever be ready?

Can you ever know what you're getting into?

If you did, you might not breed at all. If you had any actual sense of the requirements of raising children—not being a "good" father, just not being the kind monitored by Child Protective Services—you might pass on the experience altogether. You might opt instead to sleep more regularly and to not teach another human being how to use the toilet. In this way, the very fate of our species may depend on generational reiterations of blissful ignorance and incomplete awareness.

Perhaps the only thing you *can* know for sure, the one thing you can count on as a dad, is that you are going to do things wrong. While people are no longer asking you to please, please, please not get anyone pregnant, in other words, you are still going to make plenty of (here's that word again) "mistakes" along the way. To put it bluntly, as author Michael Chabon has written, your actions will demonstrate that a father is "a man who fails every day."

A man who fails every day. This means waking up, failing, going to bed, getting up the next day, and failing some more. Over and over again for, oh, I don't know—forever?

Such cautionary realism might seem to make things a bit easier to process, knowing that presumed error is part of the design for the project.

But it doesn't.

Even amidst all his failings, a father still feels as if he needs to succeed—not that he should succeed at failing, which makes no sense, but that he should succeed *while* failing. As a dad, he is supposed to lead by example. Even if he's fallen short of that example. And even if he continues to fall short of that example. Every day.

In many ways, this seems like a conflicted charge. Yet it also sounds refreshingly familiar, even comfortable, embodying a concession at the core of that reflexive parental proclamation favored in moments of extreme exasperation: "Do as I say, not as I do."

You recognize this expression, right? It's the one that essentially admits, *Yes, my child, I realize I'm in the wrong, but I'm also the boss—the one in control of desserts and allowances—so you need to be in the right.*

When a boy is still young and sitting in the audience, this all seems quite fishy; but when he gets older and takes the stage as the announcer, it suddenly makes perfect sense. By then, with self-awareness drawn from daily failure, he has become a dad who is able to reconcile the didactic tilt of the saying's first clause with the humility of its second. Providing balanced instruction and brash inconsistency in the same breath, this father is now able to nail the right notes without the slightest pretense of harmony, making for yet another successful day of failure.

True, it can be difficult to digest the irony at first—the way we offer social promotion from the role of lawbreaker to the rank of lawgiver; and how things are neither as they seem nor as we say—but inherent contradiction of this sort is at the heart of any human compact. Sometimes things only make sense when they don't.

WHAT TO EXPECT

[A]s we know, there are known knowns; there are things we know we know. We also know there are known unknowns; that is to say we know there are some things we do not know. But there are also unknown unknowns—the ones we don't know we don't know.

-Donald Rumsfeld

YOU MAY KNOW WHAT HAPPENS most of the time, what other people have experienced, what the normal course of events is, and so on, but you still can't really know what to expect. At least not the first time through. Once you have a second child, things are different. You are more aware of known knowns, things that are both knowable and actually known. You can also better anticipate known unknowns, or the things that are knowable but not (yet) actually known—in other words, those things capable of being known, even if we cannot or do not comprehend them at the moment. And you may even become aware of a realm of unknown unknowns, knowledge we don't even know we don't (and perhaps cannot) know.

This is the epistemology of expectation, and while I should have expected it, I didn't. Nor did I like it—all this not-knowing and not-knowing-about-not-knowing business. I like to see over the horizon, and I want a real sense of what to expect. Isn't that what all those books are supposed to be for: the ones you get at the baby shower and skim a bit but can't really comprehend because you haven't had those experiences yet?

As indicated in this book's Introduction, I had not been very involved in the planning for our first child. That doesn't sound good, but it's true. I was pretty disengaged, mostly just following instructions and surely not taking the lead on anything. Emily was singlehandedly in charge of our schedule, and she wanted to deliver Lucas during my spring break in March 2005. Thus, we started "trying" to get (her) pregnant in summer 2004.[†] (Doesn't everyone pick a preferred delivery window and work backward?)

This timeline offered a challenge, which I generally like, but I was still torn. As a man looking for as much sex as possible, I saw the chance to try—and to keep trying—as long as necessary. Emily wanted me to swing at the first pitch, hit the ball out of the park, and be done with this phase as soon as possible; but I saw an invitation to stand in at the plate, foul off as many offerings as I could, bring up the pitch count, call time, step out, adjust myself, and relish the experience. I didn't know when I might be up to bat again.

Yes, it's terrible to suggest trying not to get a hit in order to keep swinging away, but I'm a man and that's how some of us are. Which presents an obvious conflict of interest, because while a guy may accept the idea of person-making in principle, in practice he realizes conception means no more sex is required. A simple kit from the drug store is enough to authorize a shutdown of all clinical bedroom trials, sending even the most potent studs out to pasture with the rest of the beasts who've outlived their usefulness.

It's a perverse arrangement of incentive arrows if you think about it, because to "win" by a woman's standard is to "lose" by a man's. This means a rational, sex-seeking guy wants to keep coming up short in order to keep trying for as long as possible. Like, maybe ten or twenty years. Otherwise, the poor fellow's story ends up seeming something like a classical tragedy: the tale of a man undone by his own doing, banished to an identity of which he never conceived just by helping someone conceive. (Sorry.)

[†] Sometimes a couple says, "We are trying to get pregnant," even though it's really only the woman who will be getting pregnant. To be "pregnant" means to have a small version of the species in your uterus. A man doesn't have a uterus. It's nice to signify shared responsibility by invoking the "we," but the "we" isn't the one who will be enduring a painful delivery.

NOT KNOWING WHAT TO EXPECT over the course of the next few months, I mostly just did my own thing, getting updates from Emily on this or that and not feeling very invested in the success/failure we had realized. I was consumed with other matters, mostly involving work. But pregnancy was also too abstract for me to process.

A father doesn't feel any kicks inside his body and nor does he suffer dirty looks for drinking coffee. Perhaps other first-time dads had a better sense of things as they went along, but I felt disconnected. It didn't seem real to me until I could *see* something—until we went in for the ultrasound Emily scheduled for the twentieth week so we could find out the sex of our first child.

If you have been through an ultrasound before, you know the mixture of excitement and apprehension as the technician—your tour guide for the journey—takes you around landmarks that look familiar to her but make no sense to your untrained eye. Heads are pretty easy to spot, but beyond that you must squint, shift in your seat, furrow your brow, and make a few calculations on the back of an envelope to figure out what she's showing you. As her probe goes here and there, up and down, she announces, "There are some toes." Or she says, "I see a hand." Or she declares, with an unnecessary chuckle, "Will you look at *that*—it's a little penis!"[‡]

Hearing the technician counting off appendages can be reassuring—one of this, five of those—but when you don't know what to expect, you don't know whether protocol requires her to begin with the *good* news. You don't know whether she could still issue a correction, as when newscasters call a race on Election Night but then have to revise

---

[‡] Having heard news of a "little penis" twice now, I would like to ask that technicians please stop saying it that way. The adjective seems gratuitous in this context, since the penis would obviously have to be "little" to be part of such a tiny frame. And it's also somewhat humiliating to hear it said that way, because the genetic source for the baby's Y chromosome—that is, the one who gave it the penis, the penis that is so remarkably little—is sitting right there in the room.

their prediction. And you don't know whether your guide might still stumble upon something in the nether regions of the belly, like the weird guy at the beach who's always looking for buried treasure with the metal detector he ordered from a Sharper Image catalog.

All you want to hear during this session is the word *normal*. When you are still in the dark in so many ways, such an appraisal can offer comfort. While your baby may be ugly, a pain in the ass, or not very bright, at least the child will be like all the other babies.

And that's something you can prove, or at least project, with the help of the picture the technician prints for you when you leave. This image gives you something to take out of your wallet and show everyone (probably upside-down, but whatever)—which is a good thing, because people are always asking. They can tell there is a baby coming.

Or at least other women can tell. I couldn't really see any difference in my lovely wife, but female friends, acquaintances, and even strangers were regularly able to detect that Emily was with child. This meant conversations. And questions.

After hearing these inquiries enough times, you can tell that an interrogator complimenting an expectant mother on her flattering maternity jeans actually has something else in mind. She may ask, "When are you due?" but she really means: "How much weight have you gained?" She may inquire, "Are you delivering at a hospital?" but that's mostly a way of determining: "Are you having a chemical-free birth like nature intended and your child deserves?" And she may wonder, "Do you know what you're having?" but that's just how she tries to find out: "Do you know who the father is?"

Those with inquiring minds often have good intentions, but as with many things involving children, intentions don't really matter. What is asked of pregnant women can easily be spoken in one way but *heard* in another. This complicates conversations with pregnant parties, because when engaging an expectant mother, it's impossible to have her entire back-story. You don't know the lay of the land, what her biases might be, what blogs she reads, what movements she endorses, and whether she puts more faith in Dr. Spock or Dr. Pepper.

In essence, you don't know your audience—which is, or should be, rule number one when it comes to potentially controversial discussion topics. You wouldn't saunter into a Jewish deli and start asking people about a two-state solution, would you? You wouldn't raise a toast to the Queen in a random Belfast pub, right? The upside is a Guinness on the house; the downside is no more kneecaps.

IT's TRUE THAT A BIRTH PLAN (or paternity determination) may not be as volatile a topic as religious homeland or matters of self-rule, but still. If you must talk with those expecting, stick with something safer.

Like names. Names are pretty much always a good discussion topic. Small talk about them doesn't have to end in awkward silence; and parents-to-be often even delight in talking about the name they have chosen for their child. This is especially true when it comes to conveying a name's *significance*, or the justification parents have for inflicting such an incredible designation on their one-of-a-kind little human.

Perhaps you have noticed that, while America ran just fine on standards like George, Mabel, Henry, and Agnes for ages, modern parents aren't generally satisfied with traditional names. They want something different. Or as they say but can't really mean, they want something "unique."§

According to breeders of this persuasion, conventional names are uninspired, milquetoast, not ethnic enough, patriarchal, chocked with too many vowels, or in desperate need of an umlaut. Names need pizzazz, in other words—some kind of special sauce. You know, like spelling Eric as *Airrick*. Or punctuating Leonard as *Leo:nard*.

---

§ *Unique* means existing as the only one. Finding a unique name is challenging, since it involves reviewing the names of the seven billion living human beings, as well as the names of anyone who has ever lived.

While a desire for distinction makes perfect sense to parents after one too many cans of PBR at the hipster bar, it's the child who will have to make something of the wreckage. It's the child who will have to endure this creative selection on every nametag at every mixer until the end of time. It's the child who will have to belabor every roll call in every homeroom at every school—forced to say, repeat, and then spell his name for every teacher he ever has. And it's the child who will always have to explain the reason for his name.

If his parents had decided to name him John, people could assume he was designated as such in honor of the Baptist, the Lennon, the Coltrane, or the Papa. But when the boy's name sounds like it emerged from a random password generator, people will ask him about it. All the time. Every time. Until the end of time. And he will hate it—not as much as the boy in the Johnny Cash song, but close.

Mother and father might have gushed with pride whenever people inquired about their choice of name, declaring, "Thank you so much for asking! It's actually a Swahili word meaning *one who flies with toads*."

But it's the poor kid who will grow up hating toads.

And never wanting to visit Swahili-land, wherever that is.

Emily and I didn't go so far as to draft options from foreign languages, but we were just as guilty of the desire for a name that was distinctive. Or again, "different" (but hardly unique). We settled on Lucas, which gave us a designation with some family relevance, but which also allowed us to avoid problems that crop up when *last* names are deployed as first names without parents having fully considered the way the two boxes on the birth certificate will be read together.

You've seen this terrible oversight occur before, when a last-name-as-first-name is combined with a last-name-as-last-name and the result is one fantastically unfortunate complete name for a child to withstand forever and a day. Failing to appreciate the whole as substantially worse than the sum of its parts, parents in this spot inadvertently find themselves sending out birth announcements introducing the world to their new baby boy: a new baby boy who, sadly, now has a name like Hunter Fisher, White Black, Cooper Smith, Walker Tripper, Carr Parker, Moore Gore, Mason Dixon, or Johnson Holder. Names such as these are not just two last names; they are two last names that have no business being mentioned in the same breath. Think through this choice very carefully, new parents. No one wants to go through life being called Johnson Holder.

When we were expecting Wills, we briefly considered calling him Whiteley, a name with significance on Emily's side of the family. But then we thought better of it. It's a fine name, for sure, but if you look at the picture of me in the opening pages of this book, you will see why I should not have a child with a name taking any form of the word *white*. Whiteley Pinaire either signifies *n*th degree WASP or it suggests sympathy with those living on compounds in northern Idaho. Since those are both bad things, it was safer for us to go with William, the first name of both grandfathers. Even though we really only call him Wills. Just to be different.

BY THE SEVENTH MONTH, I realized I had no idea what to expect during the actual delivery. This was a known unknown. Emily was a medical student when Lucas was born, and a resident when Wills was born, so she had seen numerous deliveries in her training. I, however, had seen nothing and, generally speaking, knew nothing. Thus, Emily signed us up for a birthing class at the hospital—a decision I regretted within the opening ten minutes of the first meeting.

The session began with a video depicting alternative delivery practices. After allowing a few seconds of off-screen grunting, the camera panned to a woman lying on a red sheet. Surrounded by candles and covered in oil, despite the obvious fire hazard, she was completely nude, without any cover, exhibiting the hirsute tendencies of the 1970s, writhing in pain, and rolling around while the camera zoomed in for close-up shots. Although not ideal, this was mostly fine.

After a minute or so, the camera pulled back to reveal a man lying next to her. Although this man did not appear to be pregnant, for some reason he was also covered in oil, was also grunting (but sounding more like a seal), and was *also* completely nude and without any cover.

This was not fine at all.

Emily and I didn't come back after that, by which I mean we didn't attend the next week and didn't even return after the intermission. It wasn't like us to skip class, but this was a distressing experience. Neither one of us imagined a delivery anything like this. We didn't necessarily know what we wanted, but if there is anything good that can come from seeing a naked guy acting like a resident of SeaWorld, it was the conversation that ensued over the course of the next few weeks.

As we got into the details of things, we realized we didn't know what to expect of each other. How would we react? And what was *my* role? I knew what Emily's basic assignment was, but what's a father actually supposed to do while a mother is giving birth?

As a student of popular culture, I was familiar with the trope of the first-time dad presented on television and in movies: the guy so geeked up about his baby's arrival that he trips over things, pushes random buttons, accidentally powers down the entire hospital, and interrogates received gender assumptions by climbing up the birth canal and escorting his child into the world.

A new father of this variety—call him Camcorder Dad—(over)compensates for the indifference of his ancestors by demonstrating excessive interest in childbirth. Indeed, Camcorder Dad can even become as frenetic as the mother he is ostensibly there to calm, posting live blog updates by the minute, uploading real-time video footage between thrusts, and holding a microphone to the mother's face while peppering her with sideline-reporter questions, such as: "How does it feel to be giving birth today?"; "Can you tell me what happened on that last push?"; and "I think you look great and all, babe, but—and just one more time—what's your plan for losing the baby weight?"

It's also possible that the Camcorder Dad look is just as unflattering as the one it was meant to retire: that of *Mad Men*–type guys, fathers of a prior generation whose role involved not being involved at all. In that earlier era, when all men wore dapper hats and took the train to work every day, a new father might come by the hospital at some point, as long as it didn't interrupt his three-martini lunch or post-lunch meeting with the secretary, but he wouldn't do anything except read the newspaper and hand out cigars. It was the rare man in those days who found himself wondering how he could "help." Research even indicates that delivery rooms and labor-floor environments were designed so as not to accommodate fathers in the first place.

By contrast, dads in the present day and age hear that they should be "supportive." Yet they may not understand what that means. A guy can feel he should be doing stuff, and might even want to do stuff, but he's unlikely to know what stuff to do. Being supportive is an attitude, not a set of tasks; a disposition, not actual directions. It's too imprecise for the approximately 101% of men who have ADD/ADHD or other attention disorders that exist but have yet to be named.

And, of course, all of this assumes a man's assistance is even *desired*. Who wins when the mother for whom a father is supposed to be doing something wants him doing nothing at all? This was an unknown I came to know very well, because, as Emily saw it, there wasn't anything I could do that she couldn't do better herself.

What would I add other than agitation? She wasn't opposed to me being in the room (although, for the record, nor was she a vigorous advocate of that); but she was adamant that I not hover over her, that I not act poised to catch something, and that I not lead her in exhalation exercises. And we both knew it would be a bad idea for me to gush about how "beautiful" she looked during labor, since I probably wouldn't end up sounding very sincere in that appraisal.

For my part, I was pretty sure I wouldn't gather everyone around for a speech about the "Circle of Life" or any other family-movie leitmotif, because that's not really my way. And nor would I offer up indiscriminate platitudes: neither proposing that "Everything happens for a reason" nor pointing out the obvious for everyone in the room by announcing that "It is what it is"—because, frankly, no one should ever say those things.

So, what was left?

What other kind of "help" was there?

Eating the placenta?

No thanks.

Still without any (approved) ideas as the date approached, I was nonetheless confident I could rise to the challenge. I planned to meet the moment with grandeur and grace. And I felt prepared to play the right role on the biggest stage.

Clearly, I had no idea what to expect.

THE BIRTH PLAN

But Mousie, thou are no thy-lane, / In proving foresight may
be vain: / The best laid schemes o' Mice an' Men, / Gang aft
agley, / An' lea'e us nought but grief an' pain, / For pro-
mis'd joy!

-Robert Burns

LUCAS ANNOUNCED HIS BIRTH PLAN at about eleven o'clock on a
cold night in March 2005. In a manner that signaled the personality that was to come, he offered only a few light kicks that seemed to
say: *Hello, Mom? Excuse me, but I would like to come out now.*

Or maybe the kicks were saying something else. It was hard to tell.

We had been drifting off to sleep in the basement of a friend's
house where Emily was living during her final year of medical school,
but Lucas's late-night communiqué now had us wondering what to do.
Should we go to the hospital right away? Wait for an hour? To return
to the theme of the previous chapter, when you don't know what to
expect, you don't know what to expect.

A recent visit to Emily's obstetrician let us know that Lucas would
be coming soon, probably in the next few days; but even with that
knowledge, I still found a way to be completely stunned and utterly
worthless in this moment. Emily paced the room in discomfort, while I
just tried to stay out of her way. I hoped to somehow lead by following, which sounds interesting but actually makes no sense.

After several minutes of uncertainty, I grabbed a few things, mostly
the wrong things, and drove us to the hospital where Emily was a medical student. She was feeling more pain by the minute, but all I felt was
annoyance as I stopped in the Emergency Lane in front of the hospital
and was immediately confronted by colorful language from security
guards who made it clear I could not stop there for even a moment.

Believing we had a decent case for emergency treatment given that one human being was currently trying to crawl out of another, I pointed toward the passenger seat and did a bloated-stomach impression with both arms. At this, the main guard relented with a conciliatory wave and moved on to shout at the next car carrying people who hoped to become patients.

After helping Emily get into the hospital, I went back to park the car—on the street, where it was free—and returned to find her on the labor floor. She was about to receive a long needle to the back, so I just stood there—watching, waiting, and wondering whether this was going to leave her somewhat less agitated. Eventually, she seemed slightly more comfortable, but still not herself. And her new self, or her temporary self, was doing all sorts of things I didn't appreciate. Such as not smiling her wonderful smile, for example, and also acting more erratic and unstable than I had ever seen.

Worse, there was a look on her face that suggested she was about to start changing the birth plan, adding provisions we had never discussed. So far, I was honoring my part of the plan—or, I should say, my part of *her* plan—by not hovering, not waiting to catch something, and not putting on an exhalation clinic. Yet now her wild eyes were hinting at new prohibitions—like, for example, how I should perhaps leave the state for an extended period of time. Starting right away. And how I should maybe even no longer be a living human being.

What was happening to my sweet wife, the love of my life?

As I GOT IN THE WAY OF EVERYTHING no matter where I stood in the delivery room, I realized I had to prove my worth and justify my place in this process. And so, while Emily grimaced, shifting her weight from one butt cheek to the other, I came up beside her and gently stroked her hair.

I knew this would help, because she always likes having her hair stroked. I wasn't trying to braid it, or even reattach the strands that had fallen out in the last few minutes; I simply wanted to show my devotion with an affectionate gesture. I was sure this would be a winner.

And yet, this was definitely not a winner.

Women are such strange creatures. One minute, they're murmuring, "I like it when you touch me there," and the next minute, they're giving you a look that shouts: *DO NOT TOUCH ME THERE!*

Seeing the glare that followed my helpful gesture, I pulled my hand away, trying to figure out what had happened. Emily could not have reacted that way simply on account of being touched, because *everyone* was touching her for one reason or another: brushing alongside her, poking her, bumping her, prodding her, and lifting her. She had been a veritable touchscreen since the moment we arrived.

I briefly wondered whether she just didn't want *me* touching her but then concluded she had simply overstated the point with her eyes. It was probably the hormones. Definitely nothing to do with me.

Feeling emboldened by this middle-of-the-night leap of logic, I responded with an open-handed caress of her head, sweeping away yet another large pile of recently shed hairs in a manner that asked, *Not even like this, darling?* I was sure this would be a winner.

And yet, this too was definitely not a winner.

STOP IT! her frustrated face said. *DO NOT TOUCH ME! DO NOT TOUCH ME ANYWHERE!*

I'm sure she doesn't mean—I thought to myself, before she shot me another look, this one demanding: *AND DON'T BREATHE ON ME, EITHER! YOUR BREATH STINKS!*

While the ban on touching was reasonable, the breathing-prohibition seemed petty. Shuffling off to a corner of the room, I felt self-conscious and wondered if I should go down to the gift shop to buy some mints.

AND ALSO, she added, finding me with her eyes while I tried to hide behind some kind of strange device hanging from the ceiling, *DON'T BREATHE ANYWHERE NEAR ME!*

Oh, thanks, I thought. *Am I allowed to breathe at all?*

It's a question that I genuinely wanted to ask but also didn't—mostly because she might mull over her response longer than a loving wife should, but also because every time I made any eye contact with her whatsoever she added new stuff to the list of things I couldn't do.

Like, for example: *STOP LOOKING AT ME! NO MORE LOOK-ING AT ME!* Which is a command she issued even when I wasn't really looking at her, because I actually couldn't see very well around the strange device hanging from the ceiling. I was running out of ways to help, and I still hadn't actually helped in any way.

What else was she going to add to the birth plan without my bless-ing and without any prior notice? And what's the point of even *having* a birth "plan" if it's going to change by the minute? This whole thing seemed more like a birth *whim* to me, which is a really good point I was about to make before Mount St. Emily erupted once again, grunting in extreme pain and harnessing all that energy toward me with a roar from her eyes that insisted: *STOP TALKING TO ME!*

Huh?

AND DON'T EVEN TALK ABOUT ME!

If you're scoring at home, I was now prohibited from touching her, breathing on her, breathing near her, looking at her, talking to her, and talking *about* her. By process of elimination, all I could do was stand off to the side, stare at my shoes, and exhale into my shirt.

This was not how I had envisioned the delivery. Still, what options did I have? On the one hand, I resented this treatment. But on the other hand, it *was* her body. Meanwhile, on a third hand borrowed for purposes of discussion, what kind of precedent would this set? What would it mean for our next child? If I didn't want my role limited to recovery-room visiting privileges, I needed to right this ship. And soon.

Desperation being the mother—or, in this case, the father—of invention, I turned to the fleet of nurses and asked *them* what I could do to help. Though slightly subversive, since I was undercutting Emily by offering assistance to the *other* women in the room, these ladies were in charge. The head nurse, in particular, was sympathetic to my plight. She had seen this sort of thing more and more lately: fathers showing an impulse toward involvement without having the sense to know whether they were part of the solution or part of the problem. And having witnessed perfectly normal Emily's perfectly normal meltdown, the boss was able to offer me wise counsel.

"Reach out and take her hand," the head nurse said, looking at me like an acting coach who has just asked her student to fall backward during a team-building exercise. "And while you do that," she added, "talk to her in a soothing voice."

"Oh, come on!" I scoffed. "I don't even do that in real life."

Do it, her face said, portraying both patience and annoyance.

While I doubted this idea would work, especially since it violated the bans on both touching *and* talking, I waited until Emily's eyes were closed, gently grasped her hand—or at least a finger or two—and prepared to whisper something soothing, like maybe the lyrics from that song about the man and woman who discover they both like drinking piña coladas and getting caught in the rain.

Yet as soon as she felt my touch, Emily shot me her most aggressive glare of the night. My face mused, *Wow, isn't it funny how things work out?* Her face said something different: something unprintable.

As we both looked toward the head nurse to learn what was supposed to happen next, the rest of the nursing team began working with bedside mechanisms that they called *stirrups*. I'd never heard that word used outside an equestrian context, so at first I chuckled a bit. But after I recovered, the head nurse asked me to help move Emily's legs into these devices—which I did, first repeating the directive out loud, just to make it clear I was only following instructions, and then retreating to a different corner of the room (one without a strange device hanging from the ceiling), from which I could watch the delivery and resolve to have a better plan next time around.

Plan B

WHEN WILLS CAME ALONG three years later, I was ready. By then, I realized my only job was to get us to the hospital. With Lucas, we—which is to say, *I*—had been clumsy and confused; but with Wills, the process would be streamlined and efficient. Bags packed, egos checked at the door.

Based on his antics in the womb, punching all the time and trash-talking his human host, Wills indicated he would be the type to escape in a hurry. Which he did, beginning on a Sunday night at about ten o'clock. In the dead of winter and on one of the coldest and windiest nights in years.

Emily tried to downplay the pain at first, resisting going to the hospital for fear of false alarm, but I knew this was it. Wills was banging on his cell like an inmate in the prison psych unit. Since we had no time to lose, I called my parents to watch Lucas, took charge of the situation, and essentially kidnapped my wife.

Leadership requires bold action.

Despite continued resistance from the pregnant party, I got us to the hospital as fast as I could. Not the one where Lucas was born, because we had moved to another city after Emily was done with medical school, but still a facility that seemed fine. It was pretty close to our house, and, even better, it had a free parking garage on site—a free parking garage I was headed toward until we drove by the front door of the main building and Emily yelled, "STOP!"

"Here?" I replied. "Are you crazy?"

Perhaps *crazy* is not the best word to use in conversation with a woman in labor, but this was outrageous. As Emily explained with some grunts, she wanted me to use the valet service—wanted me to walk over to the guy in the heated booth who had shown no interest in helping anyone and then wanted me to tip him for all his hard work.

"No way!" I said. "*Our* spot is in the garage, up two flights, and near the service elevator. Sit still. We'll be there soon."

Or at least that's what I *tried* to say, even if I couldn't actually convey that message, because, by then, Emily was expressing some of her own leadership through bold action—shaking her head in disgust as she got out of the car and hobbled toward the door. This was a woman who had taken an oath to honor and protect me, but that wasn't the vibe I was getting at the moment.

I hurried out of the car and tried to make it look like I was helping her, although now she was walking faster just to get away from me. A staff member saw this interaction (or lack thereof), helped Emily into a wheelchair, shot me a disparaging look, and whisked her off to the labor floor. Or whisked her somewhere, I guess, although we still aren't sure where. Somehow, I managed to park the car (in the free garage), walk into the hospital, get lost, get help, get lost again, and still arrive on the labor floor before the woman who was actually in labor.

It's possible the staff member was just confused, perhaps thinking a female patient holding her belly and wearing pajamas might have come in for non-emergency Botox injections, but this uncertainty and diminished sense of urgency ended up being something of a problem. Wills was coming very soon. On a standard clock and with a standard child, the delay probably wouldn't have mattered.

But Wills is not a standard child.

ONCE EMILY GOT INTO A ROOM, we hoped things would improve. Yet the nurse, who claimed to have been working on the labor floor for fifteen years, could not get an IV into Emily's vein.

She tried. And failed. And tried again. And failed again.

She blamed the needle. She said the air was too humid. She said the air was too dry. And she said Emily's skin was too taut.

I realize phlebotomy has its challenges, but Emily is a skinny gal, with veins like the ropes longshoremen use down on the docks. I wanted to lift her lovely wrist, introduce it as Defense Exhibit A, and point to the blood visibly coursing along under the skin.

"Am I going to get my epidural?" Emily asked, her voice quivering as the nurse continued to struggle with the IV.

"Well, I don't know," the nurse responded, after several moments of no response at all. "I may need to call in the stick team."

"The stick team?" I repeated, since I like to repeat things that sound funny.

"Yes, the stick team," replied the nurse, annoyed by the tone of my repetition-as-question. "They are who we call to stick problem veins."

"Problem veins?" I repeated, because, well, you know.

The irony was overwhelming. As an anesthesiologist, Emily administers epidurals all the time. She believes in them, promotes them, was happy to have one when Lucas was born, and wanted one as part of her birth plan for Wills. But she knew an IV was a requirement in this process, a necessary first step still not taken.

And soon it would be too late.

She was near tears, as was I.

Well, I wasn't really near tears, but I was upset. This time, I thought we might actually stick to the plan; I thought we might draw a nurse who knew how to do things you learn on the first day of nursing school; and I thought we might have a conflict-free delivery. I had been doing my part (nothing), but now it looked like Emily was not going to get the medicinal mojo that had helped with her part last time.

While the nurse came by every few minutes to see if the stick team had arrived, we sat there in an uncomfortable silence punctuated by loud grunts. Until a small man entered the room with no introduction.

"You must be the stick—" I surmised aloud, figuring it was possible the team had turned into a solo enterprise.

The small man neither confirmed nor denied any stick-team association, but he did raise his palm to indicate there would be no more talking at this time.

"Am I going to get my—" Emily tried to ask, only to be rebuffed with the same hand gesture barring all future questions.

"I am your obstetrician," the small man finally announced, once he was good and ready.

"No, you're not!" Emily fired back, drawing on years of experience dealing with patronizing male doctors.

"Well, I am tonight," he clarified, sounding surprised that a woman would realize he was not the obstetrician she'd been seeing for three-quarters of a year.

He then pulled up a chair in order to remain as comfortable as possible for the next few minutes, told Emily to push, signaled to me with instructions to cut the cord, handed off Wills to a different nurse who had just arrived, billed an insane amount of money for all his hard work, and moved on to manage the delivery for another lucky lady who had never seen him before.

As Emily recovered in bed, I made my way over to the little box where Wills was already howling. He had rushed into the world with such ferocity that modern practices and mediocre personnel could barely keep up. And by thwarting the carefully considered analgesic strategy of his medically trained mother, he had forecast the kind of boy he was going to be: the kind for which there can be no plan.

FAMILY LEAVE

But even if mothers are more naturally inclined toward nur-
turing, fathers can match that skill with knowledge and
effort.

-Sheryl Sandberg

W HAT ARE THE CHANCES Socrates ever changed a diaper? He is
considered a "great man" in the western tradition, a figure of
profound historical significance, and yet he was also the father of a few
sons. Was he "great" with them? When he wasn't busy walking around
asking a bunch of important questions, did he help out with the kids?
Was he involved in raising them in any meaningful way?

We probably have no way of knowing the answer to this, but
doesn't it seem hard to imagine? Can you really picture *Socrates* wiping a
baby's butt with leaves, linens, or whatever Athenians used in the fifth
century BC? Can you envision him singing "Perseus Had a Little
Lamb" to appease a youngster who wouldn't eat his bowl of figs? Do
you think he would have cancelled an appointment with Plato so he
could see one of his sons' wrestling matches? Would he have taken the
day off from philosophizing in order to stay home with a sick little
Lamprocles?

While we're at it, consider other great men throughout history. Did
Julius Caesar, Charlemagne, any of the kings of England, Thomas
Jefferson, or Abraham Lincoln read to their kids at night? Did they
remember their birthdays and give them piggyback rides? Did they take
the children to a pasture and pick dandelions with them? Did they play
games, roughhouse, converse, and have a close relationship with the
little ones? Or were the kids the sole responsibility of the Mrs., the
Queen, the First Lady, the helpers, the handmaidens, or various other
caretakers?

Such significant historical figures are special cases with remarkable resumes, for sure, but even ordinary guys have *some* ambition, some sort of meaningful legacy they'd like to leave. How, though, is that done within a conventional family context? If a guy has some kids, and he wants to be a part of their lives in a lasting way, how does he also pursue his other ambitions—especially ambitions that require all or most of his attention? In short, if he wants to be a great dad, how can he also be a "great man"?

Being a father takes commitment, will, initiative, and time: resources and energies that must be drawn from some other source and likely some other pursuit. With only so many hours in the day, days per annum, and years in the span of childhood, how does one "balance" work and life in this way? Is it even possible? Just how involved can a father really be if his job requires him to cross the Rubicon, serve as Holy Roman Emperor, behead a bunch of wives, conjure up truths that are self-evident, or free the slaves and wage civil war?

Mother Nature

THESE ARE THE THINGS that I thought about during the family leave I took with Lucas. Obligations were pulling me in competing directions as I tried to reconcile being a new father away from his job with being a man who felt he should be—and often even preferred to be—at work instead. While I was officially relieved of many professional responsibilities during this semester on leave, I was, at that early point in my career, still untenured, anxiously seeking a publisher for my first book, and nervous about what the next few years had in store.

At the same time, I was also trying to learn how to handle a six-month-old baby, struggling to feel enthused about my new role, and seriously wondering how I was going to manage either work or life once I went back to full-time teaching. It was a disorienting period when I had time on my hands but no energy; when I hoped that I was doing something good for the future even as I felt totally lost in the present; and when I was looking at my watch all the time and wondering what one does with a baby at ten o'clock on a Tuesday morning. Even to *me*, this seemed like a time of day and day of the week when a man should be at work. I eventually came to appreciate the opportunity to take family leave, but the experience was far more difficult than I had expected. And I won't pretend it was entirely positive.

Primarily to get us out of the house and enjoying some fresh air, but also to keep myself from getting sucked into another fascinating episode of *Regis & Kelly*, we went on lots of mid-morning walks around town. This let me take care of a few errands, and it opened my eyes to the ways a man is perceived when he is toting a baby around. (Toting a baby around like an *egg*, perhaps? Yes, like an egg. Good question.)

As usual, Lucas would be dressed in an androgynous "onesie" plus the sun hat that Emily wanted him to wear even on drizzly mornings. Meanwhile, I would be in my uniform of running shoes, baseball cap, cargo shorts, and a funny t-shirt that only five percent of the population would understand—completing the profile of a new father with spit-up stains on my shoulders and bags under my eyes indicating I was no longer on speaking terms with that thing known as *sleep*.

But best of all, while also worst of all, when we went around town, I would have Lucas attached to my torso by way of a Scandinavian-sounding device, a BabyBjörn, that had him facing outward, ensuring he would draw in passersby with his large eyes and perfectly shaped head. (You can see from this picture that I'm not exaggerating about those eyes or that head.)

I never liked the attention we got when I wore this thing, but it was the easiest way to get Lucas from one place to the next without having to take him in and out of the car. Guys driving by in work trucks would laugh and point, but I got used to the abuse. Eventually. What I could not accept, however, was the presumption of incompetence that I noticed on these outings.

As a straight, white, upper-middle-class man, I was unaccustomed to finding identity a barrier to involvement. I wasn't used to failure being assumed before I even had the chance to screw up on my own. And I was not expecting to have so many people be so surprised to see a man out in public with a baby. Without a mother to help. Without a nanny to offer advice. Without a net to catch what he was sure to drop.

Perhaps the sight of a guy wearing a baby on his torso at ten o'clock on a Tuesday morning doesn't, or wouldn't, strike you as a remarkable sight, but this was in 2005, and things were different back then. Plus, at the time, we were living in a region of the state that tended to be more culturally conservative and committed to traditional gender and parenting roles. On campus, the reception I got with Lucas was one thing; in the community, it was quite another. Spectators just didn't know what to make of us. Lucas wasn't usually crying or fussing on these outings, and neither was I, but those whom we encountered were frequently curious and occasionally concerned.

THE CHECK-OUT CLERK at the drug store would size me up in line, smile at Lucas, and then ask, "So, I guess Mom is sick today?" Even though we were neither buying cold medicine nor picking up a prescription, she always assumed that "Mom" must be ill. Why else would Lucas be with *me*? Apparently, a dad on the field had to mean a mom on injured reserve.

The reaction was about the same at the library, where the librarians would say to my little guy, "Hello, sweetie! Is Daddy babysitting you today?" I knew what they meant; but at the same time, I didn't. When a woman has a baby in public, is *she* presumed to be "babysitting"? Or is she just being a mom? These librarians were just making conversation, of course, and were probably happy to see a father doing something— anything—for his child, but the framing of the question is indicative of a larger problem. It reinforces the notion that a baby is essentially the mother's responsibility, and it suggests that a father is simply filling in: that he's a babysitter, as it were.

That word gets used a lot in situations like this, actually, but—and setting aside the inherent bias in the question—does it even make any sense? How does one "babysit" one's own offspring? Babysitting is when you pay a teenage neighbor to sit at your house and watch television while your kid is asleep upstairs. If someone wanted to hire me for ten dollars an hour and offer free Wi-Fi for the evening, that would be one thing; but until that deal was on the table, I wasn't a babysitter. I was just a parent. Just a dad. Just a guy looking for some respect in an endeavor I thought society was supposed to reward.

I would look for refuge at the park, where I often saw other fathers on weekends; but at mid-morning on a weekday, it was only a circle of moms (or nannies). I would be pushing Lucas in the swing or going down the slide with him, but the moms (or nannies) would always be watching with palpable apprehension. Always looking over in that way people do when they're trying not to look. Always with fingers poised to press 911 on cell phones in fashionable baby bags. And always whispering among themselves, wondering, "Why isn't he at *work*?"

Seeking relief at the coffee shop, I would inevitably draw the barista who offered to add some whipped cream earmarked for Lucas, assuring me, "It's just in case he cries for his mommy." The gesture was nice, I guess, but who wants whipped cream in their black coffee? And which was worse: the fact that she really thought I might let an infant lick that white gooey mess from a steaming cup of liquid or the fact that she assumed he would clamor for his mommy in the first place?

By the time that we reached the grocery store on these outings, Lucas had inevitably drooled through the front of the Scandinavian-sounding device, as well as the supplemental towel I sometimes remembered to bring along, and he would be about to initiate his usual late-morning diaper disaster. Which would be followed by his usual late-morning meltdown unless I changed him right away. This had me agitated and desperate to get in and out of the store as fast as possible, meaning I would be frantically parsing the baby aisle looking for the special type of nipples preferred by extra-hungry infants who insist on chugging their milk and who get really pissed off when the flow stops for even a moment.

I always thought it was bad enough just writing the word *nipples* on the shopping list; but when we were in the store, I also had to read the fine print on the packaging, apply a sniff test to the rubbery contours, and even massage some of the options just to make sure they had a life-like feel. Not surprisingly, these antics brought me even more unwanted attention. It's hard to fly under the radar when you're standing around fondling latex replicas of a woman's body parts. And it's also hard to avoid scrutiny when your partner keeps moving his head around in the BabyBjörn, batting his large eyes at a distinct class of admirers—admirers we will call Ladies of a Certain Age.

These women were at the grocery store on what seemed like a daily basis, pushing carts in formation and wearing a grandmother's uniform of faded cotton dresses and heavy wool overcoats. They would often be talking about knitting, cooking, or Eleanor Roosevelt, but those conversations would stop whenever they saw a baby. Ladies of a Certain Age love babies, and whenever they see one they want to gaze upon, touch, and perhaps even hold the little one. This is especially true when the baby appears to be in the sole custody of a man.

In the too-cool-for-school markets of Brooklyn or Berkeley, where all the food is both gluten- and flavor-free, an unassisted father might be an unremarkable thing. In those environments, a man would only stand out if he'd forgotten to wear his beard, flannel shirt, or Converse shoes. Or if he didn't bring his own bags.

But we were not in one of those environments; we were in a smallish town, where the population—especially the older female population—could not process the sight of a man with an infant. For them, it was unnatural: like a cat fetching the newspaper or a teenage girl reading a Robert Ludlum novel.

And so, when the Ladies approached, always with a look of *Where is that baby's mother?* on their faces, I would explain that Emily had since returned to her job, and that it was now my turn to handle childcare responsibilities during a three-month family leave from work. But whenever I got to that part of the story, the part where I used the word *turn* in this context, they would reply with an expression asking: *Turn? When did people start taking turns?* Which was followed by another look, this one wondering: *And, goodness, what on earth is a family leave?*

Clearly, this was a lot to take in. These women were socialized in an era when all a man did was make some sales calls, play golf, drink, carouse, go to the track, drink some more, and then die. A father rarely did anything domestic in those days and nor did anyone expect him to. His role was limited to putting food on the table and a roof overhead. A dad could take his son to a ballgame now and again, or maybe show up sober for his daughter's dance recital, but it's just as possible all he did for the kids was destroy their self-esteem.

In that light, it's easy to see why the Ladies of a Certain Age assumed I needed help, why they always reached out to take Lucas from me, and, perhaps, why he so willingly went to them. They'd had a lot of experience and knew what they were doing. Whereas, I hadn't—and didn't. While the other fathers of the world were busy pushing paper around, swinging hammers, and driving things that make a beeping sound when you go in reverse, I was maneuvering a cartload of nipples and a boatload of self-doubt.

At first, I resisted offers of assistance from the Ladies—too proud to admit that my method of bouncing up and down while desperately shushing Lucas wasn't really soothing him at all. But then I relented. And watched. And learned. Slowly, but surely. I didn't get good instincts from Mother Nature, so I was determined to make up for it with Father Time. Lots of Father Time.

Father Time

DURING MY SECOND FAMILY LEAVE, this one with Wills, in fall 2008, I had a much better time of things. Wills was definitely a challenging baby, even more so than Lucas, but my prior experience left me feeling I could handle the charge. It also helped that, by this point, we had moved from that smallish town to a suburb near a large city. We were now surrounded by more families with arrangements like ours, situations where both parents worked outside the home but where one had a more flexible schedule.

In this new environment, I could take a baby and a three-year-old to conventional kid locales like a children's museum or zoo at ten o'clock on a Tuesday morning, perhaps see a few other dads there, and generally not get any looks of concern. Or maybe I *did* get looks of concern but just didn't notice them anymore. Either way, it felt like progress.

I was still outnumbered, of course, as the majority of parents at conventional kid locales at mid-morning on a weekday were still women, be they stay-at-home moms or took-the-day-off-work moms. But these women were different from the kind I encountered when Lucas was a baby. These were Ladies of a *Younger* Certain Age.

Mothers of this vintage still noticed an unassisted father like me, for sure, but they rarely seemed alarmed at the sight. One guesses this is because they grew up during a time when movement in this direction was already underway: a period of increasing fluidity with respect to household assignments and family arrangements. These women perhaps still hewed to more traditional roles in their own homes, but those in their cohort were generally aware of other possibilities. They may even have had sisters, friends, or frenemies whose husbands, partners, or associates picked up the kids from school, did a load of laundry, or made dinner once in a while.

Often wearing a uniform that included Uggs and yoga pants, Ladies of a Younger Certain Age moved in packs, were regularly immersed in conversations about the flaws of other mothers, and tended to push strollers overflowing with provisions. This had them carrying every article of pacification they might need to manage a tantrum, stashing organic carrots for toddlers who couldn't go ten minutes without a snack, and storing an array of maps, flashlights, and radio transmitters that would come in handy during the next earthquake.

The upside of this tendency, this phenomenon of overflowing strollers carrying everything in the world, was that Ladies of a Younger Certain Age were carrying everything in the world. That meant they always had Neosporin at the ready, even before their kids got a cut. And they were even willing to share some of those organic carrots with other—ahem—*less* prepared parents, like a certain father who might have "forgotten" to pack snacks that morning.

But the downside of this tendency, this phenomenon of overflowing strollers carrying everything in the world, was the same: they were carrying everything in the world. So much of everything in the world, in fact, that young aristocrats were often ousted from their chariots— obliged to walk alongside the cargo of coloring books, first-aid kits, comestibles, and stuffed animals lovingly packed on their behalf.

Such intense preparation is good in some ways, because it's nice to have things when you need them, but it can also go too far. Like, for example, when it's mostly just an effort to out-mom the other moms— a contest, in some sense. Or when it breeds a self-reinforcing expectation that a "good" mother must be ready for anything, must anticipate every danger, must foresee every emotional turn, and must do it all in a seemingly effortless manner that makes other mothers think: *How does she do it?* And also: *I totally hate her.*

FATHERS DON'T HAVE THIS FIXATION, this sentiment that makes them feel the need to be Superdad: a man who makes things right before they're even wrong. Or at least I don't feel that need. And nor do any of the dads I know.

Granted, the sample size of men doing much or most of the childcare is smaller, but dads seem less inclined to turn parenting into a competitive sport. As more fathers manage trips to conventional kid locales in the next generation, maybe they will move in the direction of Ladies of a Younger Certain Age, feeling as if they are supposed to do things in a particular way because (they think) that's how everyone else is doing it.

Or maybe they won't. Maybe dads just aren't wired that way. Maybe they approach parenting in a qualitatively different manner.

It's a generalization, for sure, but your average dad is a simple creature—one who understands that men in earlier eras were able to create entire empires with as little as a machete, a 9-iron, and a flask of whiskey. One of these average dads can handle an outing to a conventional kid locale, but he's unlikely to arrive (by choice) with a stroller overflowing with provisions. An average dad doesn't need that much for a trip to the zoo. Walking around for an hour looking at monkeys is not the same as preparing for a journey along the Oregon Trail.

An average dad brings the basics on one of these trips, like the children, but he probably won't pack anything more than can fit into the pockets of his cargo shorts. That's why he wears those things, you know—for function. (God knows it isn't for style.) An average dad loves pockets; and in those pockets, he only wants to carry instruments that are easy to implement and multifunctional. He favors accessories that mirror his own rudimentary but eminently capable form. He wants equipment that is small but can do it all: tools that offer maximal utility with minimal hassle. Tools such as hand wipes.

Yes, hand wipes. Hand wipes are like a Swiss Army knife, except that they don't have a corkscrew. Or blades. Or that toothpick no one really uses, because it's kind of gross.

While you may scoff (go ahead and scoff), devotees of hand wipes put them on the list of greatest human innovations somewhere between the wheel and Pop-Tarts. Not only do they facilitate cleanups on the fly, but they're also a substitute for tissues during cold season, they're able to absorb a surprising amount of blood, they will occupy a frustrated toddler for hours when he's been challenged to fold the soft square of wet fabric into a paper airplane, and they can deliver a fantastic array of chemicals in the war against entire races of bacteria.

One cannot overstate the importance of portable sanitation on an outing with little people, particularly since children recognize personal hygiene about as much as Attila the Hun respected human rights. Trained observers at conventional kid locales see this problem with every visit. Despite piles of germs large enough to be visible to the naked eye, youngsters make it a point to touch everything, lick their fingers, touch everything again, lick one another, and then touch everything one more time.

Back when I was just a man, not a dad, I never cared much about this stuff. But by my second family leave, with a toddler always getting his baby brother sick, I became a believer. Father Time made me more aware of child-spread threats to public health, turning me into a germ-fighting gunslinger at the O.K. Corral: a self-deputized agent willing to arrest an unsuspecting (and even unknown) youngster running by with a face slathered in goop and a dad drawing moistened munitions from my cargo shorts with a sense of mission strong enough to foist one of those wipes upon any child—mine or yours—who needed it.

To return to the spirit of our question from the outset of this chapter, can you imagine *Socrates* doing something like this? I mean, can you really see him standing tall while stooping over to wipe a youngster's face? Can you envision him doling out hand wipes to children instead of dispensing wisdom to the world?

Probably not.

Is that because this isn't the kind of thing a "great man" would do?

No, of course not. It's just that togas don't have pockets.

THE DESCENT OF MAN

Among the men in our sample who were single nonfathers as young adults, those with higher waking T [testosterone] were more likely to have become a partnered father by the time of follow-up. Once these men entered stable partnerships and became new fathers, they subsequently experienced a large decline in T, which was greater than the comparably modest declines seen in single nonfathers during the same period. Finally, fathers who were most involved in childcare had lower T compared with fathers who did not participate in care.

-Lee T. Gettler, et al.

HAVING SOMEHOW SURVIVED WARS, substances, disease, and crime, a man approaching middle age finds his maleness turning on him. Or just turning off. Known as *Manopause*, this is the unfortunate phase of life when a guy begins losing testosterone in earnest, feels his libido dropping, sees his muscles deteriorating, has less energy, seems like a wimp, and brings it all home by growing man boobs.

A man (or whatever) in this position can still use the men's room for a while longer, but it's only a matter of time. Nature is taking him downhill, and children hasten his descent. Especially if he has anything to do with those children, since—as the epigraph to this chapter suggests—fathers more involved in caring for their kids have lower levels of testosterone than fathers without involvement.

To be clear, *all* dads (and all men, generally) are drifting toward the same eventual destination; it's just that those serving up some chicken nuggets and sitting for tea parties earn a gust of wind pushing them across the line even sooner. A guy in this spot knows he is breaking down, that nature is spiriting away his essence, but your average dad is probably unaware that nurture is complicit in the shakedown. He doesn't realize that the little people walking around the house making noise, messes, and trouble are actually sleeper agents executing stealthy hits on his masculinity. They may appear drawn to him, but that's just a ruse to get the proximity necessary to bring him down and turn him out once and for all.

So, what's a man (or whatever) to do? Try and contain the damage? Sure, but *how?*

By doing push-ups, buying a Harley, and starting a brawl?

Perhaps. But will that really help? He has so much to overcome.

For example, did you know that research shows fathers who are more involved with their kids *also* tend to have both an increased body mass index and diminished testicles? What model of Harley will melt away his belly flab? What are all those push-ups going to do for his small balls?

A man (or whatever) in this position should feel both trapped and duped. He should be outraged by a swap he never sanctioned. He should be chagrined by a switcheroo that is both out of his control and of his own doing. He should be up in arms. He should be pissed off. He should stop finger-painting, trade in the minivan, and start a war.

But he won't.

How could he throw down the gauntlet if he can't even lift it?

And how could he remember to start the revolution when he now forgets everything? New fathers tend not to realize how bad things really are, because the mind is slipping as fast as the body. Some of this can be attributed to a lack of sleep, which research shows reduces one's IQ, but there are also deficits that come from time spent talking in silly voices, setting up puppet shows with socks, and suffering the subliminal assaults embedded in children's television programming.

Just as much, the adult mind finds itself compromised by kids' books. A new dad isn't reading those highbrow works he used to savor: no more erudite tomes on astrophysics or the Atkins Diet for him. No, now the best he can do is a scratch-and-sniff story about a little red dinosaur who feels scared on his first day of Jurassic preschool.

At a certain point, a new dad isn't even smart enough to realize he's become stupid. People look at him with pity, but he just assumes he has a piece of food in his teeth. He doesn't understand why they feel so sorry for him, because he's past the point of understanding much of anything at all. It's like showing up to work one day and getting a note that says: YOUR SERVICES ARE NO LONGER NEEDED—but then losing the note before you leave the building and continuing to show up to work every day because you've forgotten you were fired.

And it's also like writing a book about being a dumb dad and jotting down notes all over the place, but then losing all those notes because you put them in a folder for important notes—before forgetting you *had* a folder for important notes, then wondering where all the notes went, and eventually forgetting you had any notes in the first place.

And then forgetting you were even writing a book.

But then remembering about the book and shifting over to digital notes to make things easier—before getting really annoyed with all the text messages you were sending to yourself, wondering, *Why the hell do I keep bugging me?*

And, finally, deciding against writing a book about turning into a dumb dad, because, obviously, you wouldn't know anything about that.

Wait, what was I saying?

SOME FATHERS PUSH BACK against this conspiracy of nature and nurture, this assault on body, mind, and manhood itself. We call them Alphas. Other fathers threw out their backs lifting a toddler into his high chair two weeks ago, so they can't push much of anything at all. We call them Betas.**

** While there is a degree of correspondence between the more generic term *alpha male* and the notion of an Alpha as used here (as well as *beta male* and Beta), the dad-iterations speak only to the situation of a man who has *already* become a father, thus shifting his position to a new category, lifestyle, and set of considerations altogether.

Sometimes Alphas have Beta moments (when no one is watching), and sometimes Betas find themselves with Alpha urges (because it's how they used to be), but a father tends to settle in as essentially one or the other type. Alphas mostly look for ways to avoid interacting with kids and the associated descent of man, while Betas mostly embrace children and a thoroughly revised construction of manhood itself.

Alphas don't want to tend to the kids, because they are too busy tending to themselves. They have little ones at home, little ones they were happy to create, since that part—the *creating*—makes them more Alpha-ish. Yet they don't do much for those kids, since that part—the *caregiving*—makes them less Alpha-ish. As it suits them, Alphas might mingle with their progeny if, say, they want to demonstrate to the youngsters how good they are at racing cars, climbing mountains, and picking up chicks. But that's about it.

Quality time with the kids isn't their thing. Their thing is swinging on this, swiping at that, growling here, roaring there, thumping their chests, and generally having their way with the world. The children are okay every once in a while, but an Alpha basically expects them to be the responsibility of Mrs. Alpha, or one of the Mrs. Alphas.

Alphas rationalize this lack of engagement as a means of steeling kids for battles ahead, a way of preparing them for life. They don't feel disdain toward the small people; it's more that they just want and even need to be detached from them. Alphas recognize supremacy through strength, bending reality to their will, and they know nothing comes to the weak except an early death.

It's a jungle out there, and Alphas always have other Alphas coming at them. Plus, they have seen the research referenced above, demonstrating that as interaction with kids goes up, testosterone goes down. In the interest of self-preservation then, Alphas maintain both physical and emotional distance. Consider it a law of nature.

Betas see things differently. They aren't natural enemies of Alphas, but that's because Alphas would never view them as a threat. To the extent that Alphas consider their counterparts at all, beyond simply laughing at them, they imagine Betas living a caged existence, trapped within the obligations of family life and unable to fly around like a "free bird" (the Alpha mascot).

A Beta doesn't deny his relative confines, but he prefers to think of his "cage" as a *voluntary cubicle living unit*—one from which he is free to leave at any time, by the way, perhaps to go to exciting places like work, a child's soccer practice, or the occasional fantasy football draft party. A Beta knows he would have to check in at some point during that draft party, and that he certainly can't fly away, but that's okay. He doesn't want to be a free bird. (At least not all the time.)

Indeed, attachment is what defines him as a type. A Beta genuinely enjoys his youngsters and tries to view his relationship with the kids more in terms of opportunity than obligation. He doesn't *like* changing diapers or dealing with temper tantrums, because no human being does, but he might enjoy coaching some sports, going to school events, and generally being a part of even the mundane daily matters of life with children. Perhaps he never imagined this as his future, but Beta-ness can sneak up on a man like that.

And it can also make him see things quite differently. By shifting his position on the road of life (to the carpool lane, of course), a dad of the Beta persuasion is able to zip past all of the Alphas who are revving the engines in their turbo-powered pickup trucks but still going nowhere— mostly because their lane (the passing lane, of course) is jammed up with too many other Alphas headed to the track, the mountain, or wherever people go to pick up chicks.

While a Beta will concede that racing cars, climbing mountains, and picking up chicks is still a fine way to spend the day, that just isn't his thing anymore. When the kids came, he changed; unawares at first, but eventually with acknowledgement. And ultimately with endorsement. Consider it a law of nurture.

The Björn Identity

THE DIFFERENCES BETWEEN Alphas and Betas may not be evident at first glance. Indeed, both types of dads may dress poorly, be equally obnoxious, and drink the same kinds of beer. Upon closer inspection, things like sippy cups and car seats are often a giveaway, but nothing screams "Beta" louder than the decision to wear a BabyBjörn.

Betas who have been "Björned" have the best of intentions, motivated by the research-demonstrated benefits of this sort of intimacy, but they either don't know or don't care that, as they walk along, they are leaving behind a trail of testosterone like Hansel and Gretel dropping breadcrumbs. Every time a Beta puts on one of these things, which takes about an hour because of all the stupid straps and clasps, his supply of this defining male hormone dips to ever-lower points. This is the Grand Canyon–deep descent of man.

Wearing a BabyBjörn lets a father feel a baby's movements, observe the child's developing awareness of the world, and whisper bits of social commentary into captive little ears. All good things, for sure. And yet, this man still looks absurd. He does. You know it.

 Whether the child is facing in, and thus drenching the man's shirt in drool, or facing out and smiling at the world, a guy can't look right when he's imitating a kangaroo—especially since only female kangaroos have the pouch he's trying to replicate.

It can be rough walking around the airport or the shopping mall while wearing one of these things, but Björn-Man (or whatever) can generally handle stares and snickers. What he cannot get used to, however, is finding himself in a simultaneously strapped-in *and* filled-up position. In other words, having a small person suspended in the air just above the anatomical fixture essential to the evacuation of his bladder.

Yes, we are talking about peeing.

Yes, we are still talking about wearing a BabyBjörn.

And yes, I'm sorry, but we *are* talking about peeing while there is a baby in that BabyBjörn.

When nature calls, what is nurture supposed to do? What options does this guy have? Would you rather he placed the baby on a shelf next to the toilet plunger while he took care of his business? Do you think it would be better if he approached a stranger in the bathroom and said, "Hey dude, I gotta piss—can you hold this thing for me?"

No, he couldn't ask that terrible question, and nor could he accept the help of a man who would agree to that in the first place. Guys don't "hold" things for other guys in the men's room. Never. This is black-letter law.

The only option here is for Björn-Man (or whatever) to stay in straps as he empties out—which is gross, to be sure, but also more challenging than you might think. Not only is a guy unable to see his unit with a baby in the way, but it's also quite likely this affair will be marked by numerous violations of international men's room norms (beyond just having another little person hanging there).

For example, while an adult male knows a urinal user is allowed no more than a slight turn to the left or right, perhaps to acknowledge the comments of another urinating party, an *infant* male doesn't know this rule and will almost certainly turn his head beyond the allowable amount, drop his gaze below the socially acceptable horizon, and then emit a *splehhhhhhhhhhhhhhhh* sound at full volume.

And there's no coming back from that.

Björn-Man (or whatever) can't just say, "Sorry, he has allergies." He can't pretend the sound actually came from someone battling diarrhea in one of the stalls. And nor can he simply bolt out the door—because, remember, *he* still has to pee.

When this kind of thing happens, which is more often than anyone wants to admit, a man-in-straps might hope to chat with his passenger about this infraction, offering some advice to avert therapy down the line. But he can't. At that moment, he has other pressing concerns.

As soon as he leaves the men's room, he has even more shame to endure. He still needs to get home, which means he still needs to walk by that construction site that's always in his path no matter where he goes: a construction site that's always stocked with Alphas, Alphas with pictures of his image as target photos on their spittoons.

Björn-Man (or whatever) hates the looks these guys give him as he cruises by at one mile per hour, but he's unable to do much about it. He can't speed up, because the baby's head would hit him in the chin, which actually kind of hurts. And he can't even use his hands to shield his face, because the baby likes to hold his dad's thumbs as they go along, pretending the digits are joysticks and laughing hysterically as he steers them both into signposts and mailboxes. This always causes the Alphas at the worksite to take a break from doing nothing at all in order to enjoy a hearty chuckle. It's not every day that you see a mock marsupial walking by, especially one that appears to be drunk.

Our hero, the one bravely toting a baby and sacrificing himself for the cause, might try to feel better by recalling that these extra-manly Alphas are the same guys who arrive at the construction site sitting three-across in the cab of a pickup truck, situated surprisingly close to one another for such large, sweaty men. And, even more, he could snicker at the thought of these same large, sweaty men reaching through airspace only inches above the middle guy's crotch in order to tune in some country music before a long day of standing around in a circle.

But is that enough? Does it even things out?

Probably not.

Still strapped-in in so many ways, all Björn-Man (or whatever) can do is proceed with care past all the workers, accepting acts of feigned goodwill as they tip their caps toward him in the same way they would for a little old lady. He would like to offer the same gesture in return, if only to indicate surrender, but he can't. Don't forget—the baby is still holding his thumbs like joysticks.

Shop Class as Fathercraft

SOME AMOUNT OF ALPHA OR BETA identity is programmed from the start, but the remainder of a man's paternal form is waiting to be determined by habits, occupation, family, community, circumstances, and, in some cases, training. Ideally, this training would occur as a built-in element of a young man's life, offering him the chance to pick up some skills, cultivate some sensibilities, and bone up on the stuff dads are supposed to know. If we had something like this, we would call it Dad School, and it would probably spawn a moderately funny movie of the same name. But we don't. Instead, we have a class in real school: a class called Shop.

You remember Shop, right? With the intention of building young men into young men who could build, Shop was one of those classes that always seemed to forget education is wasted on the young. The sad fact is that thirteen-year-old boys can't really learn how to build much of anything when they're surrounded by other giggling idiots who lose it every time the teacher says the word *wood.* Or *nuts.* Or *screw.* Or *nail.* Or even *hammer*—because of, you know, M.C. Hammer.

This is the age when boys mostly just focus on how to have even worse body odor, how to fashion regrettable hairdos, how to avoid initiation rituals involving toilets, how to take a shower in the presence of other males, and various other elements of the school experience that resemble a prison sentence.

And as if the above were not already enough to discourage learning in any form, an unfortunate educator's discourse on vise-grips could never hope to compete with those images, symbols, and codes carved into the wooden benches that accent any given Shop space in any given junior high/middle school anywhere in the galaxy. Exhibitions of adolescent angst in classes like Home Economics (Home Ec) could be somewhat deterred by the slippery surface of laminate countertops and modulated by the pacifying aroma of slow-baking banana bread, but Shop was a complete anarchy of disregard and devastation.

Worst of all, Shop actually armed its aggressors with the very instruments of their terror, offering sharp tools and idle time to lads fixed on destroying the wooden benches at which they sat. Boys doing everything except learning how to build stuff thrived at furniture vandalism and reveled in deciphering the carved-in contributions of prior generations of students who had sat on the very same stools, destroyed the very same benches, and ignored the very same teacher.

The most active carvers at our school belonged to a tribe we called Hessians. At the time, it was unclear why they had this name, since, technically, the term refers to German soldiers hired by the British to fight during the American Revolution. But in retrospect, perhaps it's because our Hessians were their own kind of army: joined with one another in their collective affinity for long hair, black t-shirts, torn jeans, white high-top sneakers, and chains connecting their wallets to their belts, while also showing a group-consistent commitment to the mission of getting in fights, smoking in the bathroom, shouting at teachers, and expressing their considerable and perpetual rage with a screwdriver during each and every Shop class.

The topics of their carvings varied, but most of the caricatures and commentary pertained to either heavy metal bands (especially Quiet Riot) or girls in our school—including girls in the local area and girls who were at one point in our school or in the local area. In particular, Hessians liked to immortalize the phone numbers of certain debutantes known to provide a "good time" for anyone who called, debutantes named Tammy (or sometimes Cami) who were always willing to "give head."

Back then, *give head* meant . . . well, you know.

While information such as this amounted to a valuable life education all on its own, every once in a while, our teacher, who we referred to as Mr. Crackly Hands, would bother us with assignments. He had visions of us all becoming roofers or mechanics, capable members of the working class. And he talked a lot—preached, actually—about how we needed to build things if we wanted to grow up to be real men. (He said this to the girls in the class as well.)

For Crackly, working with one's hands was the very essence of manhood, and any self-respecting male had to know how to force stuff together, pry it apart, cut it up, and screw it. (Cue giggling, every time.) The problem was, Crackly didn't really like teaching. Or kids, for that matter. He grumbled a lot, was prone to outbursts, didn't appreciate smart-aleck comments, and went apoplectic when we weren't wearing the "safety" glasses required by the school district's insurance policy.

The glasses looked stupid, for sure, at a time in one's life when no one wants to look stupid; but they were also so loose they wouldn't stay on your face. And even if they did, they were so scratched and cloudy you couldn't even see things right in front of you. They were more like blinders, actually—and blinders are not what you want on your face when you're running a jigsaw you don't really know how to use, because Crackly didn't show you how before he once again left the room to "get something from the car."

Not surprisingly, as creatures interested in keeping our fingers, most of us removed these glasses in order to actually see what we were cutting. Yet this was always the exact moment Crackly would return, have a fit, and make us stop working on not really making anything in order to *again* watch the video about the boy who gets his eye poked out while playing with an awl.

Following this, we would be punished with probationary projects designed to keep us busy for the rest of the period, such as assembling small boxes made of balsa wood—boxes where, as Crackly suggested, we might keep our "snuff." Even though no one knew what snuff was.

One kid at our bench said it was a type of movie, but no one believed him. Who could fit a VHS tape into a box that small? Besides, this was the same kid who claimed to have had a good time with Tammy (or sometimes Cami)—which I knew was bullshit, because I'd already called all those numbers and they were out of service.

MANY YEARS LATER, when the balsa-wood box is sitting in your attic, probably inside some other dumb box, and perhaps holding the gym bag you sewed in Home Ec—the one big enough for only one shoe— you wish you could go back to Shop and pick up some of those skills it seems dads are supposed to have.

Now you are finally mature enough to get something out of a class like that. Now you might even have a garage, space for a workbench, and a smattering of tools. And now your kids want a tree house—a tree house that you have no clue how to build.

Well, to be clear, a *Beta* has no clue how to build that tree house. All he can assemble is a paper airplane and a bowl of SpaghettiOs. Which he is reminded of whenever he goes to the hardware store and all the Alphas who work there ask if he needs any help locating the batteries or house plants. Still, a Beta who's realized that all things can be learned—like fatherhood itself—might just give it a try.

Raising a tree house won't be easy for him, and it will take ten times as long as it would for an Alpha, but a Beta with perseverance might somehow end up with a structure safe enough for mammals larger than squirrels. He can do some research, draft plans, ready his workbench, gather his equipment, don a tool belt, secure some safety glasses that actually fit (as well as a pair in a smaller size), scope out a tree in the yard, look down at the little boy who is always looking up to him, and say, with hope in his eyes, "Hey pal, how about if we build it *together*?"

PATERNITY CHALLENGES

Maternal gatekeeping is typically defined as a collection of beliefs and behaviors that may inhibit a collaborative effort between men and women in family work. Specific gatekeeping behaviors can include assuming primary responsibility for childrearing tasks or criticizing the father's actions when he is involved. Mothers may engage in gatekeeping behavior for a variety of reasons, including a belief in the appropriateness of differentiated family roles, the need for validation of a mothering identity, a pessimistic assessment of fathers' competence in child care, or the adoption of particularly high standards for child care.

-Sarah Schoppe-Sullivan

D ADS NEED A MASCOT. They need something to represent them in their various capacities: from protector, teacher, and coach, to playmate, friend, and confidant. A dad is used to finding his identity in teams, clubs, and groups—used to cheering for this set of uniforms to beat that one, or for these colors to blot out the other ones—so he will be comfortable falling in behind a symbol.

It just needs to be the right one.

Humans seem to gravitate toward emblems from the animal kingdom, but let's make one thing clear from the start: dads cannot be tigers. Tiger Dads will not work. The image is too freighted. For one thing, Tiger Woods is still out there, somewhere—still trying to resist the allure of pancake waitresses and still watching out for golf clubs coming toward his head. But for another, tigers are now linked to a certain form of motherhood. Tiger Moms are their own thing, with their own identity, values, and resulting hullaballoo.

Lion Dads is an option. Lions are a good model for us as fathers, because they're strong, powerful, wise, and committed to protecting the pride. They also seem to make good kings, even if they *are* susceptible to assassination when their asshole brothers get a little power-hungry. We don't want to walk around with a target on our backs (or tails), so we'll probably need to find something less famously associated with fraternal skullduggery.

Wolf Dads is an idea to consider. Wolves look creepy, for sure, but they are cunning, relentless, and similar to dogs (i.e., man's best friend). At the same time, we would get some resistance if we had a wolf image on our chests. People don't think too well of the species, which isn't surprising. It's hard to build a campaign around an animal best known for terrorizing a little girl in the woods and then eating her grandmother. And let's not even start on how the three little pigs were just trying to build their houses in peace until *someone* kept coming by and causing problems.

If you believe the Hollywood propaganda, you might think that Penguin Dads would be a good choice. But it wouldn't. That's not a knock against penguins; whether ruling the South Pole or playing hockey in Pittsburgh, penguins are great. Still, we won't be able to sell human males on this pairing, because while a penguin mother is off gathering fish or shopping, a penguin father mostly just stands around in the bitter cold for hours while balancing an egg on his feet. Other than standing around in the bitter cold for hours before a football game (which is totally different as long as you don't really think about it), this is not something human dads are inclined to do.

The affection of penguin fathers is endearing, but the one-to-one ratio they use for watching over eggs is too cumbersome. If those birds had some consultants come down to Antarctica, they would realize it's far more efficient to stop with the parallel parenting and instead work out a system where the dads put all the eggs in one big pile and then take turns standing guard against predators.

This sort of pile-them-up approach encourages self-sufficiency by forcing the eggs to keep *themselves* warm, given that—as long as they manage to stay intact, of course—the ones on the bottom of the pile have several other layers above them to create and maintain warmth. Meanwhile, the ones on the top could learn important lessons about the randomness of life. More importantly, this arrangement would let penguin fathers get some shut-eye, take a run down the glacier, and then play a game where they throw bags of dried corn into a hole.

Some human dads might urge us to consider mascots that look cool on the Discovery Channel, like sharks or Komodo dragons, but let's wait on those two. Yes, they are tenacious and come across well on the screen, but do we know how they are as fathers? What if they do their thing—biting surfers and whatever it is dragons do—but *only* their thing? What if they don't help out with the little sharks and dragons? What if their behavior out in nature is incommensurate with our own aspirations—or the aspirations we aspire to have one day? We don't want to be tied to something that makes us look even worse than we manage to look on our own.

For our best bet, we need to think outside the mascot box. We need to be released from convention, open to big moves, and willing to take bold steps. We need to free our minds. We need to realize a way to be somehow invincible in our vulnerability. We need to fall in line behind a creature that sounds ridiculous. We need to go with titi monkeys.

Never heard of titi monkeys? Good, then you can't be biased against them. Well, you can be, but don't. Research indicates that titi monkeys are highly involved fathers from the very beginning, carrying their offspring ninety percent of the time after birth. This early commitment—attachment, if you will—means that baby titi monkeys become more upset when separated from their fathers than their mothers. Can you imagine that?

Sure, we could have some trouble getting human males to fashion themselves after monkeys, especially since it seems to be going the wrong direction in the evolutionary sequence, but that's where the marketing comes in. That's where we have a big dad-bonanza and roll out t-shirts with **T I T I** written boldly across the chest.

Get it? Human dads will love it! It's such a dumb gag that dumb dads will end up wearing these shirts every day, chuckling at the boob joke every time they look in the mirror but still feeling obliged to live up to their mascot's high standards.

Titi Dads. Who's with me?

Make Room for Daddy

SINCE THE RELEASE of the film *Mr. Mom*, dads have been subject to a terrible stereotype just for doing things like making sandwiches and throwing a child's baseball uniform into the washing machine. While this movie was obviously a satire, it reinforced the notion that kids, home, and the like are a woman's (a mom's) responsibility, meaning that a man (a dad) who happens to be the one taking care of things for the household is not simply an involved father, but is instead a male-form mother. Or, in other words, a "Mr. Mom."

And an idiotic one at that.

This movie wasn't the first entertainment offering to send such a message, and it won't be the last. The notion is, in fact, pervasive. Scroll through your options on basic cable on a Sunday afternoon and you'll surely find some movie about dopey dads running a daycare or a sitcom portraying a father so clueless that he fails to notice *four* young people climbed into his minivan after school. Even though he only has two toddlers. And even though the two new kids are of a different race. And one of them has facial hair.

If we want to continue to view dads as hapless buffoons, incapable of handling matters in the home, sure to lose the kids and replace them with stage props, likely to burn down the house while boiling water, inclined to call the little ones by numbers because their names are too hard to remember, and so on, that's fine. We'll get some laughs out of it. And yet, we'll also be indicating our assent. We'll be affirming a certain vision of domestic affairs and essentially using as our guide the arrangements of the past rather than the potential for the future.

But if, instead, we want to shed the shackles of presumptive dufusness, resist clichés, and actually resemble the realities of modern family life, we must locate and expose these tendencies, renditions, and caricatures wherever we confront them. Perpetrators need to be called out and made to account. In the same way that racism is all around us even though no one thinks they are racist, people hold anti-paternal views they don't like to admit—or that they rationalize by relying on outdated conceptions of domesticity.

To fight back, we must fix our attention on the media, on the entertainment industry, on corporations, on service providers, on marketers, and on ordinary conversations with ordinary folks. It's time to make room for daddy. There's plenty of space at the table.

MY FIRST ENCOUNTER with anti-paternal energy occurred at our pediatrician's office when Lucas was a baby. This office was mostly fine, with the exception of one nurse who refused to concede the changing nature of the American family. Every time I took Lucas to an appointment, which was virtually all of them, the substance and tone of her questions wavered between mild disdain and unequivocal hostility. She wanted nothing to do with fathers. In this way, as I think you will see in the stylized composite transcript below, she set back our movement with her every word.

dramatic re-creation

The scene is the examining room of a pediatrician's office. Having already waited patiently for thirty-eight minutes in one (or both) of the waiting rooms—one for "sick" kids, one for their "well" counterparts—a father and his infant son have finally been ushered back to meet the wizard. Still, it will be another twenty-seven minutes until they see an actual doctor (forty-one during flu season). The nurse has just entered the room. It is ten o'clock on a Tuesday morning.

NURSE, *looking at a clipboard and sounding annoyed.* It doesn't look like you completely filled out our forms. You can do that at home and then mail them back at your own expense.

ME. Is that really necessary? I fill them out during every visit, and the information is always the same. How about if you just keep the filled-out forms for the next time we come in?

NURSE, *sounding annoyed.* Excuse me? You *must* fill out the forms every time. It's a rule. We give you forms, a clipboard, and a ballpoint pen in order to keep you occupied while we're running a little late.

ME. You are running a little late every time we have an appointment. Do you ever run on time?

NURSE, *sounding annoyed.* Phone number?

ME. Eight, six, seven, five, three, oh, nine.

NURSE, *sounding annoyed.* Eight, six, seven, five—wait, that sounds familiar.

ME. Say it out loud. *Sing* it, actually—and draw out the nine at the end. Really stretch it out, like *Ni—eeeeeeee—innnnnnne.* Did you grow up in the eighties?

NURSE, *sounding annoyed.* Is Mom still breastfeeding?

ME. No, we have transitioned to—

NURSE, *sounding annoyed.* You know, in some countries, children are breastfed until they are five or six years old.

ME. Yes, and in those countries, they also have famine and drought, without any alternatives. My wife breastfed into the tenth month, which is awesome, but now we use—

NURSE, *sounding annoyed and checking the* BAD MOTHER *box.* So, Mom must be feeding formula to Baby?[††]

[††] Those in the baby business prefer to drop the article before the word *baby*. It appears to signal that this party is in the know, evincing a private vernacular for nurses, lactation consultants, and others who operate under the pretense that your baby, who is also *a* baby, or even *the* baby, is generically just *baby*. Or *Baby*. Listen for it next time you are being bitch-slapped by one of the usual suspects. It goes like this: "This is what *Baby* likes," "*Baby* wants us to say it this way," and so on.

ME. Yes, Mom is doing that. But here's the funny thing: so is Dad! As his very presence before you might suggest, Dad is *also* involved. On that note, you might focus on the just-emptied baby bottle sitting in front of you. That would indicate that Dad is one of the parties providing sustenance to the child, right?

NURSE, *sounding annoyed.* How much formula is Mom using?

ME, *making the case for team parenting by throwing Mom under the bus.* Well, Mom pretty much just guesses, actually. It might be a dollop here and there; seventeen ounces on Mondays, but none for the rest of the week. By contrast, *Dad* is the picture of precision with formula. He measures every serving with a sanitized postal scale and even massages the powder to release extra nutrients.

NURSE, *sounding annoyed and doodling* I HATE FATHERS. Does Baby still go to daycare?

ME. Yes, Baby—or whatever—goes to daycare.

NURSE, *sounding annoyed.* And how many days a week does Mom take him there?

ME. Zero.

NURSE, *sounding annoyed.* Sir, we don't have time for this. You said Baby goes to daycare but then said Mom never takes him there. It's not good for Baby to be around a liar.

ME. Listen, there is another person who takes care of *Baby*, as you like to call him. And that person's name is Dad. Well, that's not really his name, I guess, but for purposes of this exercise, where we keep referring to people by their role instead of their actual name, we can go ahead and call him that. And Dad actually does things, too—like taking his child to daycare. And also to the doctor's office. By the way, do any doctors work here?

NURSE, *sounding annoyed and castrating a voodoo doll.* Next question. Does anyone smoke in the home?

ME. You mean besides Mom? I'm trying to get her to quit, but you know how addicts are. She says she can't stop with the cigarettes until she kicks her heroin habit. How about that? Is that a good thing for Mom to be doing?

NURSE, *sounding annoyed.* Have Mom call me. She needs to know there are women who can help. It's terrible that she's going through this all by herself, all day long, without anyone to lend a hand. Does she have any sisters, aunts, midwives, or other loving women to assist her? Is there anyone else in the home or in the area who is capable of helping out?

ME. You mean like Dad?

NURSE, *sounding annoyed.* No, she needs a communal sisterhood to care for Baby. They can escort her to recovery meetings in a fleet of Subaru Foresters.

ME. Fine, but who will install the car seat?

STROLL THROUGH THE GROCERY STORE and you'll see the same sorts of paternity challenges in nearly every aisle. Because dads are not often the ones filling up the cart, product messaging remains directed toward mothers. Shelves are stocked with goods reminding consumers that "choosy moms" choose Jif peanut butter, that Kix cereal is "kid-tested" and "mother-approved," and that Robitussin is "recommended by Dr. Mom."

Marketers take this approach as a way to sell more merchandise, obviously, but along the way they also sell a particular vision of the family. Perhaps a "choosy dad" just chooses whatever a choosy mom wants him to choose. Or perhaps he doesn't know what to choose. Actually, a father probably just chooses whichever one is on sale, because peanut butter is pretty much all the same. That's such a "dad" thing to do.

But peanut butter isn't really our issue here. I mean, don't get me wrong, the disrespect certainly hurts; yet it's not our main concern. Our main concern is baby-related products steered to only one parent—which is to say, only toward moms.

Certainly, some things in the baby aisle should be associated more with mothers than anyone else, such as nipple creams and MOMMY & ME memory albums. But when the product is for the *baby*, not for the mother, does it really need branding oriented only toward the female parent? Or if it once needed that, does it still?

Consider the case of diapers. It's true that mothers are probably the ones buying the majority of them; but as a commercial good, is there anything necessarily "maternal" about diapers? Isn't a diaper just the thing you put on a baby to keep most of the waste contained? And don't mothers *and* fathers (and others) change those diapers?

Why would diapers be any more effective by being linked to moms? And why would a grocery store chain promote a store brand that has essentially written fathers out of the story by declaring that mothers are the only ones capable of handling those diapers—from creation through destruction?

It hurts me to do this, like shooting a sick old dog, but Safeway, *you* are on notice. In the over sixteen hundred stores you have throughout the United States and Canada, you sell a line of baby products called "mom to mom."♯ Your website advertises these as goods "designed and created by moms, for moms," including diapers you refer to as "high quality."

As a father (I understand you don't care about me, but still), I can't tell you how pleased I was to find out that someone out there finally started making a line of high-quality diapers. If my kid is going to crap in something, I want it to be a high-quality something.

I also can't tell you how happy I was to learn of the rationale for your brand name. "As moms," you say, "we want nothing but the best for our babies," which is why "mom to mom" products were "created using the shared wisdom of the real experts in caring for babies: moms like you and me."

♯ N.B. Safeway (or SAFEWAY) portrays this brand name in lowercase letters.

Thanks, Safeway. Really, I mean that.

It's comforting to know that now the "real experts" will be (back) in charge. No longer will we have to endure a bunch of foolhardy men with pocket protectors (but no "shared wisdom") trying to cook up batches of inferior diapers. Instead, a posse of pissed off moms has been deputized to kick down the door to the lab, run out the nerds, and enforce the rule that all things baby-related must be associated with moms and only moms.

But still, Safeway, while I assume focus groups (made up of mostly or only moms) responded positively to the "moms" proposal, was it really worth it to exclude dads in this way? Couldn't you have named the brand "parent to parent"? Or couldn't you just skip the caretaker angle altogether by giving the brand a name like "best for baby"?

It's true you didn't go with something like "dads are dumb," but as a corporation, don't you exist for the purpose of making money? Shouldn't you want to sell as many products as possible? Why write off fathers with cash in their hands?

While we're at it, who was it that first suggested the idea of mom-approved baby products, anyhow?

Seriously, who pushed for this?

Wait, you know what—I bet it was *men*, right?

Maybe some Mad Men?

In fact, I bet the pitch for this concept went something like this . . .

dramatic imagination

The scene is the conference room of a large Madison Avenue advertising firm. A meeting has been called to consider new product and branding possibilities for the firm's largest client, the Safeway chain of grocery stores. The characters are the managing partner on the Safeway account, the associate partner on the account, and a summer intern who somehow slipped into the meeting. It is ten o'clock on a Tuesday morning.

"We need to boost sales," the managing partner said as he opened the meeting. "We need something new—or at least something that seems new. Who has something that is kind of new but not in a way that is at all risky or disruptive?"

Seeing a chance to finally land himself in one of the firm's prized corner offices, the associate partner on the account decided this would be his day to shine.

"I know, sir," he said. "Let's do something with baby products. Let's pretend we have come up with better diapers or something. We'll do a hard push toward parents, but really just mothers, because they'll eat this up. Of course, we'll also be sure to gratuitously use words like *safe* and *trust* in the campaign, since that trick always works."

"Hmmmm, baby products," the managing partner said, clearly taken with the idea. "I like it. It's the sort of thing that can keep us connected to this client for a long time. Babies are going to be around for a while, right?"

"For sure, sir," the associate partner replied, happy to see his boss so pleased. "Even better, we should link our products to the consumer through the brand name itself. Like, what if we called it *mommy loves you* or something like that? We'd be going for the jugular and pulling on the heartstrings at the same time!"

The executives then paused for a moment, reminding each other to take it one game at a time, to think of the season as a marathon not a sprint, to dig deep while staying hungry, to circle the wagons, and other things people say instead of actually saying something. Meanwhile, the intern sitting in the corner, the one with horn-rimmed glasses who had been working at the firm during the summer but who found the environment offensive to his more refined tastes, decided to speak up. He was majoring in women's studies at a terribly expensive liberal arts college and had been learning quite a bit over the last two months.

"Um, excuse me," the intern said. "Isn't that kind of silly? I mean, a better *diaper*? And naming the brand *mommy*-something? Even if we did make a diaper that was better, or safer, or whatever, what does that have to do with the person who changes the diaper?"

The executives sat speechless.

Whose nephew is this? they wondered. *And why is he in the room?*

Feeling emboldened, the intern closed his book on feminist theory and hit them with some more fancy talk. "Actually, guys, isn't this entire discussion pretty gendered?" he asked. "Why would someone be more likely to buy a brand just because it's got the word *mom* in it?"

"Because," replied the associate partner, "our research shows that when focus groups hear that word they think of fresh-baked cookies and hugs and kisses."

The associate partner always referenced this research, no matter what the account—even though the report was from 1953 and was based on interviews with only seven people living somewhere in Iowa.

"Yes, but what does that have to do with diapers?" pressed the intern. "And more importantly, what kind of statement are we making by sticking to clichéd conceptions of the household? Rather than taking seriously the fact that families are constructed in nontraditional ways, with gay and lesbian parents, single dads, grandparents, and so on— none of whom are moms, obviously, or at least not necessarily—we're going to cling to a notion that doesn't mesh with reality?"

This kind of incisive observation and social commentary would have gone over very well in his women's studies classes at the terribly expensive liberal arts college.

"Uh," said the managing partner, unsure how to move the ball down the field and stalling until he could come up with just the right noncommittal language to indicate he had absolutely no intention of considering the point just made. "Thanks for that, son," he finally offered. "But that field has already been seeded. So, what we'll do is run it up the flagpole and—"

"Have you guys ever heard of titi monkeys?" the intern interrupted, intending to deliver a mini-lecture on the role of fathers in the animal kingdom, before changing direction and suggesting: "Never mind—how about this instead? What if we flipped your *moms* idea on its head? We'd get a ton of publicity and also make important points about hegemony and societal biases if we did something truly original. Like, what if we came out with a brand called *dad to dad?*"

As the intern spoke, the managing partner looked up *hegemony* on his laptop, and the associate partner reached for the buzzer to call Security.

"We could pitch it as being, you know, *designed and created by dads, for dads*, or whatever," the intern continued. "Wouldn't that be fantastic? Think about the attention we'd get! Moms walking by our display in the store would be outraged, most likely, but there's no such thing as bad press, right?"

The managing partner missed most of this exposition, because he was sending a note to his secretary trying to move up his tee time. However, the associate partner had been listening intently and was now seething, since he *really* wanted one of those corner offices and his "moms" campaign was being sacked by a little punk using big words.

"Late night hosts," the intern added, "would joke that our diapers come with duct tape. They'd say our formula tastes like a cheesesteak and that our pacifiers are made from pork rinds. Just imagine the national conversation we could encourage!"

The associate partner looked like he might explode.

"Plus," the intern went on, "all of our diapers would be stocked in the cooler next to the beer! Parenting blogs would kill us for suggesting that fathers have some kind of innate advantage when it comes to taking care of children, but we could finally force some important questions, particularly regarding the ways that we, as marketers, are part of the problem. Gentlemen, *this* would raise our consciousness."

After more than a few awkward moments of silence, the managing partner said, "That's interesting." This was what he said when something was not very interesting. "I definitely like the part about the cheesesteak."

"Yes, a cheesesteak *does* sound good right about now!" the associate partner agreed, always happy to agree.

The executives then did a fist bump, and the intern finally understood why the Equal Rights Amendment never passed.

"Let's say," said the managing partner, intending to wrap up this discussion with even more nonspecific corporate-speak, "that we also run *this* up the flagpole. But not all the way up, because there's already something up there, right? After that, we can drill down a bit, smack one into the gap, circle back, give a hundred and ten percent, pressure-test the whole thing, and see if we get any pushback on the flipside."

Anyone else in the firm would have realized that a blistering array of hackneyed and utterly incompatible business-world idioms meant it was time to shut up. Yet the intern didn't care.

"I realize this is my last day here, my last meeting, and probably my last minute before I'm removed from the building," the intern said in conclusion, "but you guys keep perpetuating *Leave It to Beaver* notions during *Modern Family* times. Don't you see? Things have changed."

The associate partner went back to imagining ways to draw even more antiquated conclusions from the Iowa research, while the managing partner just couldn't stop thinking about that cheesesteak. Still, they'd both perked up at the mention of *Leave It to Beaver*. They loved that show when they were growing up and even got to talking about their favorite episodes as they left to play golf.

Meanwhile, Security escorted the intern out onto the street, where he didn't see anyone named Ward, June, Wally, or Beaver, but where he did notice all sorts of modern families walking around at mid-morning on a Tuesday.

EARLY CHILDHOOD EDUCATION

When a father teaches his little son to walk, he holds his two hands on either side, closely, lest the child fall down; but when the child is nearest to him, he holds his hands farther apart so that his son may learn to walk on his own.

-The Baal Shem Tov

FIRST DAYS OF SCHOOL can be as hard for parents as they are for kids. Kids might think otherwise, assuming parents don't appreciate their apprehension, but parents were once kids themselves, giving them a dual perspective. In such moments, adults are supposed to say that everything will be "all right"—and they're supposed to mean it. But there's really nothing quite like feeling the fear in that small hand that is squeezing your fingers for comfort as you are preparing to leave your child in a new setting.

It probably will be all right, eventually, because kids have a knack for this kind of thing. Indeed, the most precocious of them will have made new BFFs by snack time. Even the slower starters, the more reserved ones, will warm up at some point—perhaps by the end of the day and surely by the end of the week. But when do things become easier for their parents, especially parents doing a first-time handoff of a first child?

In my pre-child life, I hadn't anticipated having separation anxiety. With a kind of stupidity that was my default mode in those days, I assumed the first morning of daycare would be relatively uneventful and certainly not emotionally unsettling. Actually, if anything, I figured I would probably be trying to find ways to *exceed* the maximum number of hours allowed per day at the facility. I saw the matter as a simple transaction and was sure I would be unaffected.

One hundred percent sure.

BUT AS WE ARRIVED AT THE DAYCARE associated with the university on that first day in July 2005, I suddenly felt unsure of everything.

Our plan had been to have Lucas in part-time care for the latter half of the summer, after which I would begin my three-month family leave and then a research leave in spring 2006. There was some flexibility in this arrangement, since I would be either caring for Lucas at home or working from home, depending on the semester; yet there were also fixed elements of the schedule. I had short-, medium-, and long-term publishing requirements I had to meet, and thus daycare assistance was essential.

I knew this plan inside and out, since I'm the one who came up with it. Still, not until I walked toward the door of the facility that morning did I actually register the fact that we would be leaving Lucas in the care of others for the first time—a recognition that caused me to stop walking toward the door and, instead, stand in place like a person who's lost and in need of assistance.

After a few moments, I resumed walking—but paused again. Then I started again—but stopped again. Then I started once more—but now in a different direction. As evident from his signature earnest look and furrowed brow, Lucas was curious about all this stopping and starting, plainly wondering, *Daddy, what are you doing?*

Clearing my throat, rubbing my itchy red eyes, and trying to manage the other seasonal-allergy symptoms that coincidentally flared up the very moment we arrived, I quietly yelled at myself: "Dammit, stop walking toward the dumpster and get the hell in there!"

What was going on with me? We made our plan, and now it was time to execute. There was no other way. *This* was the way. This was our deal, and it had to work. I couldn't work without it. The version of me from a year before would have already been at the office by now.

I realized I needed to force my own hand here. Once I got in there and away from all this stupid pollen, I would be too embarrassed not to go through with the process. It's like dialing the number of the girl you like and holding the phone to your ear long enough to hear "Hello?"—at which point you *must* say something, because she has Caller ID and hanging up will make you seem like an even bigger idiot.

"Why have you not walked through that door?!" I again quietly yelled at myself, frustrated with my own stalling. I was upset that I couldn't easily manage this simple transfer-of-child, but it didn't help that Lucas was peering up at me from the carrier, now giving me another of his signature looks, this one asking, *Daddy, will you play with me?*

That look was really hard to handle. I loved playing with him, especially when we did that game where he crawls up onto my chest like a mountain climber and then looks around from the apex before his head collapses under its own weight and he topples back down to the carpet. I was about to explain that we could do that fun thing tonight, but by then his face was inquiring, *Daddy, why are you sniffling?*

I had a theory about the sniffling, but I didn't want to get into it. It was time for action: time to demonstrate the calculated temerity of a man who has decided that, while he no longer wants to fly off the highest diving board, he also can't bear the shame of backing down the ladder. In that spot, one just has to go for it. And so, with a rush of contrived confidence, I scooped Lucas out of his carrier, put him against my chest, and charged toward the door.

Fortunately, the lead teacher in the Baby Room had seen us arrive and was prepared to take pity on me. Watching from the window, she could see I needed immediate relief. After all, it *is* a bit odd for a parent to start walking toward the building, stop, start again, do a lap or two around the parking lot, talk to himself, rub his eyes, and then sprint toward the front door, isn't it?

As I got to the entrance, she said, "Good morning! Are you ready for your first day?"

I started to answer that question, assuming she was directing it to me, until I realized her eyes were fixed on Lucas.

"Well, *I'm* ready," she added.

At least that made one of us.

Following this greeting, I was reminded of the policies, received a quick tour of happy babies and Baby Room teachers, and got the kind of attention I needed even more than Lucas on that first day. I handed over the bottles, liners, nipples, and locks that had been carefully packed for him, as well as the sustenance Emily had worked so hard to pump, label, and freeze, before the teacher noted, "You know you can come visit him during the day, right?"

This had been mentioned as an option when we first toured the facility (before Lucas was born), and at that point, I'd wondered why anyone would do such a thing. But this time, I just nodded and asked, "How many times?"

Visiting Lucas that first day meant leaving the office, driving fifteen minutes, giving him his mid-morning bottle, driving back to the office, and basically getting nothing done before lunch. Still, it was worth every wasted minute. Not in a professional bean-counting sense but certainly in terms of my progression from the basic self-centeredness of a without-child life to the necessary selflessness of a child-centric reality.

It got easier to drop off Lucas during that first week, but I also had new concerns, wondering, in particular, whether I was now doing two jobs poorly rather than one job well—or at least one job not as poorly. I'm not claiming to have felt the exact concerns I had read about in books and articles—where mothers working outside the home felt torn, judged, guilty, and generally sub-par because they were not making healthy fruit tarts; or where mothers *not* working outside the home felt torn, judged, guilty, and generally sub-par because they were not making sales calls—but I was at least beginning to understand the contours of that conversation.

LUCAS ATTENDED THIS DAYCARE for a couple of years, but once Wills was born, we needed a new childcare arrangement. We had moved over an hour away from campus, in order to be closer to the hospital where Emily was doing her residency, and Lucas had been riding along on my commute. He did as well as could be expected with this, but to have a toddler *and* an infant in the backseat for a roundtrip journey of over one hundred miles per day on an almost-daily basis seemed pretty much impossible.

After researching some local options, we picked a daycare that had fresh paint, landscaping, and pictures of generic happy kids on the walls. Then we readied ourselves for another transition, and, in my case, another bout with pollen—pollen that was really, really thick on that first day (a first day for two kids, not just one) in late spring 2008.

As we drove to the new daycare that morning, loaded up with all of our first-day gear, bags of spare clothes, forms, and so on, I knew it was going to be rough. I could feel it even before we left the house.

And things didn't get any easier when we arrived and the secretary wouldn't even acknowledge our presence. At first, I thought she was just really busy; but then I could see from her screen that she was actually only doing some online shopping. Looking for pillows, it seemed. Or maybe blankets.

We looked around and waited. Three-year-old Lucas maintained a concerned expression on his face, four-month-old Wills was blithely gnawing on my jacket, and thirty-something me was somewhere in between: eager to get things going, and going well, but also somewhat apprehensive. Something didn't feel right. I actually even wondered whether I had come to the right place.

It *looked* like the facility we had toured.

And it definitely smelled like an enormous porta potty.

And there were all those pictures of generic happy kids on the walls.

But still, this was a very unwelcoming welcome.

Did the secretary perhaps assume I was here—with two kids and several bags of kids' things—in order to fix the copy machine?

I cleared my throat and said, "Hello," hoping this universal gesture would prompt her to realize we were here for purposes of childcare.

"Uh huh," she murmured.

"This is Wills and Lucas," I continued, nodding to my left arm and downward, respectively. "We're just starting here today," I added, hoping to get the help-train rolling soon.

"Uh huh," she murmured. Again.

I considered stating for the record that I was definitely *not* here to fix the copy machine, but after a few more moments of bizarre inattention, she beat me to the punch, asking, "Did you sign in yet?"

"Sign in?" I asked, genuinely needing some additional information, this being our first day and all.

"You need to sign in," she repeated.

While I stood there feeling dumber than usual, Wills made faces at the pictures of generic happy kids on the walls, and Lucas buried his head in my thigh. I didn't see a way forward. The secretary seemed to have already run through her day's supply of patience for kids and their owners. The best I could muster was an "Okay" as I backed away, intending to simply mimic the arrival routine of other parents when they came through the door.

"It's so we know you're *here*," she clarified, responding to my retreat with an advance.

I gave her another "Okay," because that seemed to motivate her last time.

"If you haven't signed in," she added, "then we don't know whether you're here."

"Okay," I said once more, sticking with a winner.

"You must sign in every day," she continued. "*Every* day. Now go sign in."

To be clear, I was totally on board with the concept of signing in— totally familiar with the two-step routine where I do x and give them y in the morning, and then we do the reverse in the afternoon. In fact, during my earliest days as a daycare parent, I even appreciated the sense of investment I felt in this system—that is, until I eventually noticed that other parents always put their initials in the wrong row (the names), or under the wrong column (the date), meaning either everyone took home the wrong kids/on the wrong days or perhaps the whole "so-we-know-you're-here" rationale was a tad overstated.

As the secretary went back to the hard job of deciding which living-room garnish to buy from Overstock.com, the mother of another day-care student came through the door. Feeling the solidarity of us vs. them, which really shouldn't be so pervasive in a place where the *them* are caring for the kids of the *us*, this mom sensed my predicament and pointed down the hall.

"You have to take them to their *rooms* to sign in," she said.

"He," she added, looking down at Lucas, "probably goes to Room Three."

I thanked her, gave the secretary an "Okay" for the road, and headed down the hall in search of Room Three.

WHEN WE ENTERED ROOM THREE, the first thing I did was look around for the sign-in sheet. I had learned my lesson and was determined to play by the rules. Finding it affixed to a clipboard hanging near the door, I scanned it for our last name.

But our last name wasn't there.

I looked again. But our last name still wasn't there.

I even looked for common misspellings of Pinaire, like Paneer, Punair, and Panera—as in the fast-casual restaurant chain—but there was nothing even close. Nothing scribbled at the bottom; no post-it notes on the cover page; and no indication that there would be any new students in the room, whatsoever.

Can you believe that?

Flagging down the first teacher I saw, I said, "Sorry, but we are trying to sign in and our name isn't on here. What do we do?"

"Oh, don't worry about that," the teacher replied. "The secretary always forgets to update the sheet. It doesn't really matter that much."

"Well, then where should I sign in?" I asked, still sticking with the secretary's version of reality.

"Really," the teacher insisted, "you don't need to sign anything. It's fine."

No, no, no, I maintained in my mind. There was no way I was going down this path. Room Three was being way too cavalier about the sign-in requirement. Rules are rules, and I insisted on signing something. Even if it was just a paper towel. Or the air conditioner. Or the teacher's hand.

"Okay," I ventured, remembering how successful that word had been with the secretary, before adding, unwisely, "but then how will you know he's here?"

"How will we know he's here?" the teacher mimicked in delight. "Well, we can *see* him, for one thing!"

As she said this, she surveyed the room, earning a few chuckles from toddlers who understood they were always supposed to laugh at their teacher's jokes. Meanwhile, I realized I was just one more in a presumably long line of distraught parents brought down by a requirement that really wasn't: a father effectively debating with his son's new teacher about whether someone is here just because you can see them.

And not only did I have even more of a bad feeling about this place, but I could sense the same concern in Lucas. He always had trouble adjusting to new things, and I could tell from the way he was clinging tightly to my leg that he was going to make that sad face he always made when I tried to leave. It was a look that inevitably kicked my allergies into high gear.

So, if this arrangement was to have any chance of working, I knew I needed some way of easing him in and making him feel comfortable— some set of toys he looked forward to playing with in there, some teacher who had a good way with him, or even just some kids I could point to while saying, "Look over there. Remember those boys? They weren't that mean to you yesterday, right?"

WHILE LUCAS GOT A TOUR of Room Three, I took the opportunity to escape. I couldn't bear his terrible *Please don't go* expression, so I just waited until he was distracted and then slithered out the door like a snake. I'm not proud of that, but nor did I have much of a choice. I still had a very long drive in front of me, and we hadn't even yet reached the Baby Room, a venue where the arrival process is more involved than anywhere else.

Babies require lots of stuff, meaning there are always many things to unload; but infants also call for a hand-to-hand delivery. You can't just set a baby down somewhere, wait until he looks away, and then slither out the door like a snake. Or at least you aren't supposed to do that.

This means the drop-off dance in the Baby Room requires a part-ner—specifically, a teacher engaged enough in the Baby Room's very purpose to stop discussing Almond Roca recipes or UFO abductions, put down her coffee, make some eye contact with parents who have arrived, and then actually welcome the clientele.

I'm not sure what we missed, what we were looking past, or what we just didn't want to see when we initially toured this facility, but on our first day—and nearly every day thereafter—we found there really wasn't all that much *care* in this daycare. And especially not in the Baby Room.

The teachers never mistreated Wills, but he also didn't seem to get much attention in there. It's not that I expected this facility to replicate the care he might receive from us, or from some other caregiver working on a one-to-one basis. I was totally aware of what goes on in a daycare, how many kids they watch on an average day, and so on.

That said, we had also experienced a Baby Room that was excellent. When Lucas had been a baby—at the university daycare—the teachers were ready for us on the first day; they always welcomed us warmly; they *wanted* to hold the children; they made a big deal out of birthdays; they treated the facility like a big family; and they even knew all the kids' names, if you can believe that.

And yet, we now had both of our children at a daycare where—well into the second month, I kid you not—the Baby Room teachers were still calling Wills by the wrong name on a daily basis.

I realize infants can tend to look the same, that lots of them lack hair and other identifying features, and that some kids might only attend one or two days per week. But, at the same time, it gets pretty old when you arrive every morning to hear: "How are we today, Wilt?" Or sometimes: "Hey there, Willie!"

Since I didn't know what else to do (correct them?, redirect their question to him in my own voice and with his actual name?), I typically answered this inquiry on Wills's behalf. "Doing well," I would generally say, since it seemed like a reasonable guess and because waiting for a baby to reflect on how he might be doing today, and to then conjure the words for a proper response, didn't seem like a good use of anyone's time.

On one fateful day though, this act of conversational interposition annoyed the lead teacher in the Baby Room. As her facial expression and body language made clear, when she was greeting whatshisname, she didn't want *me* butting in.

"Oh, I'm sorry, but have you signed him in yet?" she asked, cattily, during the handover in question, once again subjecting me to the preferred form of parental discipline at this facility.

"No, I haven't," I conceded. "Remember when I told you guys the other day, and the week before, and even last month that our name isn't on the sheet?"

The lead teacher certainly knew this, because I had informed several teachers of this fact, several times. And yet, she still managed a look of surprise before using the situation as cause to call the secretary in search of some answers. I figured this was good in the sense that it might lead to us having a place on the sign-in sheet by our third month at this daycare; but I realized it was bad in the sense that I was still left holding Wills and still unable to get on my way to work.

Having no other option, I just stood there until I heard a few other teachers in the kitchen—teachers to whom I threw my voice as forcefully as I could without seeming rude and inquired, "Excuse me, but what should I do with Wills? Can someone please take him?"

"*Take* him?" one of them responded. "Take him where?"

"Well, I need to get to work," I clarified, "and all the bouncy things are already filled with other babies."

"Um," the teacher began, looking around while still seated comfortably in the kitchen area, "just put him down over there. He'll be fine."

To help me understand the idea of *over there*, she extended her arm toward the other side of the large room.

Just put him down over there? I thought. I felt like the UPS guy dropping off a box of office supplies. The oblivious baby in my arms was smiling the entire time (of course), but I hated the idea of Wills beginning his day this way. I knew they would lay him down at some point, so he could do fun things like stare at the ceiling for an hour, but did he need to start out like that? And did they need to make *me* complicit in their concerted inattention?

The room was packed with babies that morning, and, as far as I could tell, there wasn't even any room "over there." What now? Was I supposed to put him next to the trashcan full of dirty diapers? On top of it—perhaps to contain the smell? Underneath the changing table? That space could probably hold several babies if you lined them up head-to-foot.

Having by now completed her call to the office (with an assurance that the sheet would be updated very soon), and having overheard her colleague's unfortunate phrasing of the instructions, the lead teacher took a stab at damage control, suggesting, "She means just put him on the mat in the corner."

The boss even accompanied this verbal charge with an arm gesture of her own, helping me understand a *corner* to be the place where two walls meet at a right angle.

Officially giving up on both the morning and the entire facility in that very moment, I did as I was instructed. Stepping over babies scattered about like land mines, I placed Wills on the mat and watched him look around with expressions asking: *What? The mat? Again? Seriously?* Then I whispered in his ear, "I'm sorry, bud" and once again slithered out the door like a snake.

WE WERE ONLY AT THAT DAYCARE for another couple of weeks, a remarkably short stay in childcare units of time, considering start-up costs, deposits, and acclimation issues; but the looks of the place were deceiving, and we were tired of subsidizing its deception.

Fortunately, we were able to enroll Lucas in an excellent preschool program near our home, and the university's childcare center was nice enough to create space for Wills. That meant another year or more of commuting a great distance with a young child in the backseat, but it was worth it. At least to us. As parents. Which is the whole point.

If our boys had stayed at the mediocre daycare, would their childhood really have been that much different?

Probably not.

In the same way kids have a knack for making new friends, they also have a way of adjusting to new institutions, new rules, new teachers, new norms, and so on. Lucas was on his way to that adjustment. And since he was so young, Wills had never seen any better alternative—he had never seen how well a Baby Room can function when it has the right personnel.

But *we* had. Emily and I realized the discrepancy and couldn't accept the pervasive indifference of this new facility. When your kids attend a daycare, you learn that little things matter a lot: little things like greetings, gestures, knowing names, and not treating a baby like a package of office supplies. It's an early childhood education for parents.

IN THE BEDROOM

I'll do all the work. You could even be asleep. I don't care.

-a man

THIS PAGE INTENTIONALLY
LEFT BLANK

THIS PAGE *ALSO*
INTENTIONALLY LEFT BLANK

I KNOW WHAT YOU'RE LOOKING FOR, but you won't find it here. Those pages were "intentionally left blank." Like, for a reason. What could possibly fill them? There's nothing to say about things "in the bedroom" when you have young children. The bedroom used to be a love palace—or maybe a court where one could find occasional love—but then things changed. Then it turned into just a spot where sick people gather, where victims of bullshit nightmares seek consolation, and where laundry gets folded.

It's actually probably time to retire the expression altogether. While the euphemism used to be a *nudge nudge* way of referring to intimate activities, coded language only works when you can actually remember that which it's meant to obscure: when you can still recall the thing that you're talking about even as you're talking around it. This is especially true when one member of the duo is desperately trying to resurrect those memories, while the other is definitely not.

I don't want to name any names here, so let's just say that the non-participating member is known as *She*. Any given *She* has plenty of reasons for her diminished desire while the kids are very young, such as hormonal imbalances, stress from work outside the home, stress from work inside the home, guilt, despair, exhaustion, and more exhaustion. Still, it's a safe bet that her partner is not on the same page.

He, as we will call him, has many of those same feelings, and yet *He* manages to be ready and willing any time of day. And *He* doesn't understand why *She* can't do the same. His mood doesn't need to be just right. No one needs to rub his back first, talk to him about his day, or whisper sweet nothings in his ear.

He doesn't care about smelly feet or headaches, is not concerned whether the little one is finally willing to eat his carrot purée, and believes the new noise being made by the washing machine is a fine topic for conversation some other time.

Or even never.

She wonders why *He* can't better perceive her needs at this time, why *He* doesn't have an arousal metronome measuring out his desires, and why *He* throws more tantrums than the toddler in the other room.

But *He* can't empathize with her and can't track what *She* is saying—all the stuff about the metronomes and the carrots—because *He* isn't actually listening. *He* heard something about a mood or a washing machine, sort of. But mostly, *He* was just thinking: *Are you done?* And then: *So, can we do it now?*

He understands the pace car might need to slow a bit during pregnancy, and *He* was the first one to wave that flag several months ago, when *She* was taking up twice as much space in the bed; but because *She* is now back to her prior shape, *He* is now looking for a return to some *He* + *She* activities.

He actually doesn't even care if her heart is in it. That's not one of the body parts he's most interested in, to be honest. Sure, some enthusiasm would be nice, like if *She* shouted, perhaps cheerleader-style, "Yeah, let's do this thing!" But *He* is also willing to hang around till *She* says, "Oh, fine. Whatever." Seriously, *He* is. Surrender works for him.

Clearly, these are generalizations about *He* and *She*, but an author can do that in a book. Readers are inclined to accept that which resonates with their experiences while ignoring residual overstatement. Especially ambitious writers have been able to draw contrasts so extreme that *He* and *She*, men and women, actually come from different planets—like Mars and Venus—before somehow finding a way to meet up on Earth in order to propagate the human race. And to perpetually misunderstand one another.

Live by the Sword, Die by the Sword

EMILY'S RECOLLECTION OF our time with young children is that she was always working crazy hours during the day and nursing a baby throughout the night. That meant another male had first claim to her body. Even if her spirit had been willing—which, I contend, it wasn't, but whatever—there was no way her flesh could deliver.

Eros had essentially died. Or maybe it was just hidden. Or asleep.

I tried to accept this new reality, the fact that while I wanted Emily to be on PLAY, she needed to be on PAUSE—or perhaps on that slower setting where the device is going but you can't really understand the words. I consoled myself with the thought that she wasn't so much not looking at me anymore as she was not looking at *anything* anymore. Which worked well enough—at least until I caught her looking at something; until I realized things were worse than I'd imagined; and until I saw that our problem involved *The Wiggles*, as most problems do.

You see, for about two years, we had been subject to nearly lethal doses of this television program featuring Australian entertainers. If you know this show, you will recall that the main characters—four guys dressed in bright-colored shirts—prance about the stage and drive through the countryside in a big red car, singing songs, skipping, having tea with a dinosaur, and making mounds of fruit salad.

For this, they are billionaires.

Don't send me irate letters. I know they're great. Truly great. But because we had all their DVDs, I had to hear and see them every day. Every damn day. Lucas never tired of them, even as I was totally Wiggled out. That which stimulates the mind of a toddler degrades that of his father. And also, that of his mother—which I realized one terrible night while two-year-old Lucas was winding down with his favorite episode, as Emily, pregnant with Wills, relaxed next to him.

In one of the final scenes, a supporting character known as Captain Feathersword emerged, sang some tunes, danced a jig, and waved a feather sword. I made a comment about the flimsiness of that sword, implying it could signify flimsiness in other domains. It's a man's job to talk shit about another man in a goofy costume. It's what we do, and I did it all the time. But it must have touched a nerve, because Emily came immediately to his defense.

"You know," she offered, even though no one had asked, "he's actually not a bad-looking guy."

"WHAT?" I barked, almost choking on the mac 'n' cheese I was finishing for Lucas. "Captain Feathersword is *not a bad-looking guy?*"

Emily has since tried to retract this assessment, but that's how it came out at the time. Perhaps pregnancy hormones, like alcohol, bring everything to the surface. I was stunned. I had assumed her pot wasn't stirring anymore, and perhaps couldn't stir anymore, but now I realized it *was* still stirring. At least a bit. Just not for me.

How could this be? After I had been begging and pleading for weeks, months, and even years without enough on the return side of things, suddenly some lothario comes along in children's television programming garb and steals the heart of my lovely wife? Ladies and gentlemen of the jury, we rest our case against the universe.

To be clear, I'm not questioning her appraisal. Take a minute to search for his image on the Internet. (I'll wait.) If you're into singing pirates, I suppose he's hot. But his relative appeal was not really the point. The point was, while supply was failing to meet demand in our household, the supplier was now looking into side deals with a pretend captain who wears a fake parrot on his shoulder—a parrot with whom he commiserates when he can't remember the words to a song.

Even though she was married to perfectly average me, Emily was now fantasizing about a guy who hangs out with a man-sized dog and an octopus? While Feathersword was at the helm, I was walking the plank? What could explain this?

Was it his outfit? Women *do* love a man in uniform, I guess. Otherwise unremarkable enlisted men can go a long way with some dress whites in a port city. Even lowly park rangers can get some action at the campground on a busy summer weekend.

Was it his rank? Certainly, Captain Morgan, Captain Kirk, Captain Cook, and Captain Jack Sparrow have their appeal. Even Captain Crunch has his moments.

But Captain *Feathersword?* Really?

I felt sorry for myself because someone had to.

AFTER CONSIDERABLE THOUGHT and some amount of therapy, I have come to realize—which is to say, rationalize—what prompted this outburst of lust from Emily. As research in psychology and economics indicates, humans are highly conditioned by their surroundings and especially by the nature of proximate alternatives. Individuals' preferences are framed by pressures and influences around them, leading them to compare things to one another and make relative evaluations.

For example, when you're looking over the options at a discount deli, your opinion of mystery meat **B** is significantly influenced by the appearances and scents of mystery meats **A** and **C**. Choice **B** might not be great unto itself, but the mind is evaluating it *in reference to* choices **A** and **C**. The **A** option smells bad, and the **C** possibility is too cheap, even for meat at a discount deli, so you buy choice **B**—even though it isn't necessarily what you wanted before you came in. Importantly, your decision is framed by options **A** and **C**, increasing the relative appeal of winning-meat **B**.

You can see the same phenomenon at work in the everything-in-the-world superstore. Say you spend twenty minutes looking for the baby aisle and then find yourself sizing up a box of diapers that comes with a bottle of Purell. On the shelf above the box with the Purell, there is a box with *only* diapers (no Purell), while on the shelf below the box with Purell, there is a box with diapers, Purell, and travel wipes.

Maybe all you actually need is diapers, but now you are interested in the box that comes with the Purell, because *now* you are comparing it to the one with only diapers and the other one with two extra things included. In some sense, you should just buy the box with only diapers, since that's all you wanted when you arrived; yet now you realize that spending just a little—but not a lot—more will get you at least one bonus item. (If they're smart, they'll call it a "gift.")

So, what do you do?

As marketers know, many in this position end up buying the one with the "free" Purell, because they feel like they're getting more, even though it's more of something they didn't want in the first place. The box with *two* bonus items might still cost too much, but the middle option—on the middle shelf—looks more enticing than it otherwise would because the one on the top shelf "only" includes diapers.

When we apply this understanding to the Feathersword controversy, we can see that the attraction Emily felt was only an evaluation of Feathersword vis-à-vis the other Wiggles and supporting cast members. Which is to say, she was asserting a reasonable, albeit still unsolicited, preference based on her captive position from the couch—one that found Feathersword to be "not a bad-looking guy" *as compared to* the other characters who appeared in the episode.

If she'd had the hots for Jeff, the one who always falls asleep, or Murray, the tall guy with the red shirt, that would have been harder to accept. But I could see Feathersword winning this contest. He was the best of the mystery meats: the diapers with the free Purell.

Seeing the light in this more favorable way also helped me make sense of my own ~~obsession with~~ reflections on Daphne from the *Scooby-Doo* cartoons. You remember Daphne, right? She was the one who was hot—or the one I would say was hot if it were okay to say animated girls are hot. She wasn't on the level of Betty or Veronica from the *Archie* comics, but Daphne was definitely easy on the eyes. Especially when the gang was in Hawaii and she was flitting about in that bikini.

For a long time, I felt bad about rewinding the tape to watch those parts over and over—something Lucas never understood, since the plot wasn't really that hard to follow—but by thinking of things in terms of mystery meats and boxes of diapers, I eventually realized I was really only ~~in love with~~ pleased with the appearance of Daphne *as compared to* Velma. You remember Velma, right? She was the one who was *not* hot—not hot in an absolute way, not hot in a relative way, not hot in any way.

Sure, she was the brains to Daphne's beauty, but did they even need brains for that show to work? And did they actually even need to be detectives? Weren't all the mysteries self-solving? If you already know how it will end, can it even be a "mystery"? Should the gang instead have been called Foregone Conclusion, Inc.? Has there ever been an episode that did *not* end with a disgruntled guy (or gal) saying, "I would have gotten away with it, too, if it wasn't for you meddling kids and your dog"?

In the next reboot of this franchise, which they do pretty often, I would suggest they make Velma more like Mary Ann from *Gilligan's Island*, with Daphne as the obvious Ginger. That way, *Scooby-Doo* could do for amateur sleuthing what *Baywatch* did for lifeguards.

The Golden Years

IN A MATTER OF YEARS, none of this will matter. The bedroom will be freed of squatters, all the cold and flu bugs will have been flushed from the infirmary, the kids will be all grown up, and the nest will be empty. Yet while opportunity will have returned, ability will have departed—or at least diminished, as the parents are now older, broken-down, x units heavier, y units balder, z units more shriveled, less acrobatic, and probably managing a trick knee.

The de facto bedroom embargo will have been lifted, but the parties will no longer be capable of trading goods. The strike will have been called off, but the union will have disbanded. The blockade will have been broken, but the ships will have sunk. And activities "in the bedroom" could now resume if only a man were not effectively bedridden.

Back when he could have been hard at work, he found the door was often closed. But now, even as the sign by the bedroom might occasionally be flipped to OPEN, the poor guy can't see it, because he can't find his glasses. Nor can he hear of the grand re-opening, because he can't figure out how to adjust his hearing aid.

Worst of all, he may realize that the piece of equipment he needs most for the job is now in a state of disrepair: he may find, in other words, that his tool below the belt now works about as well as the crap available for rent from the hardware store.

A man can get one of those neck-chains so he always knows where his glasses are, and he can have his hearing aid permanently set to maximum detection, but if he is to find a way out of dysfunction junction, he's going to need a pill. This is America, and that's what we do.

Which you know from the commercials. You've seen them many times and have probably chuckled a bit even though they don't technically have a punchline. They can be aired at any time of day but are notably frequent during football games and broadcasts of the evening news, times when older men are likely to be watching television. And they can advertise a variety of drugs, which can get confusing, especially for older men. But that's okay, because the options are pretty much all the same. And so is the pitch.

It starts with some background music while the camera pans to a man, normally a white man in his late fifties or early sixties, although his age is ambiguous for marketing purposes. He is outfitted in a smart Lands' End sweater or some other knitwear just right for afternoon delight. It might be a Tuesday or a Saturday, but it really doesn't matter, because the whole point is that the pills can deliver, as the voiceover guy assures us, any time the "moment" is right.

And the man will know when this moment arrives, because while he's raking leaves or some other unconventionally erotic activity, into the frame walks his mildly saucy, vaguely menopausal wife (or mistress). She sidles up to our hero and gives him a playful look that says: *Come here, you.* He appears to remember that look from long ago, although it could have been a different look—or even a different wife (or mistress). He's getting awfully forgetful these days.

To help jog his memory, the enchantress grabs the rake from his hands and burrows into him. She tries to rake a few leaves of her own, which makes them both laugh, because she's not even doing it right. Nobody rakes leaves by pushing them. But no matter—the message here is subliminal: viewers see her grasp the handle and realize this guy is going to get some—that the moment must be right.

This man is as ready for business as a guy can be while wearing a Lands' End sweater and doing yardwork. And his partner certainly seems willing and able. Now he just has to hope the pills will be there when he needs them.

To be sure, it was embarrassing asking his doctor if Erectolotz was right for him, whether it could resuscitate the vitality he once possessed but then lost like a ballpoint pen. Yet now all that shame was about to pay off, and he didn't even have to visit one of those websites advertised in spam emails—the ones delivering pills from countries that don't even exist. No, this man has a bottle of legitimate chemical assistance and is all set to roll around in the leaves for a few minutes with the Lady of the Rake.

Which he does—we are left to presume, since the commercial ends before the ad turns into geriatric porn—and which was probably a very good time for him.

Or at least we hope it was a very good time for him.

Like a very, very good time for him.

Because now he's got a problem.

Like a very, very bad problem.

What sort of problem?

Oh, how to put it?

Well, let's just say that while Erectolotz *was* there when he needed it, now it won't go away.

Do you understand the problem of which we speak? This man is now dealing with a consequence that the advertisements obliquely refer to as a "complication." I'm sure you're aware of these sorts of complications. It's often the only part of the commercial anyone remembers: the somber warning at the end advising a man to call his doctor if he has an erection "lasting longer than four hours."

Doesn't *that* sound complicated?

It's not clear how Big Pharma set the line on this event—how, in other words, *four* hours became the tipping point for a problem erection, as opposed to three, two, or even one. Such a duration of erectile tenure seems excessive even for a lazy fall afternoon spent raking three or four leaves per hour. Don't people have things to do?

Certainly, Casanova knew this was a risk going in, but no man thinks it will actually happen to him. He's flummoxed and even somewhat fearful. How is he supposed to manage this sort of side effect? What does he do with fabricated wood when he's already finished the project—and when he still has three hours and many minutes to go before his problem is even clinically considered problematic?

The vixen who got all this started in the first place certainly isn't sticking around during his recovery phase. She's off to her book club meeting to drink wine and not really say anything about the book. But he's stuck at home.

Obviously, he can't go anywhere. If he set foot off the property, he'd be arrested. Sure, he could tell the officer about the rake, the wife (or mistress), the pills, and how the moment was right. But the cop would just laugh, as he should, and put the guy in jail—and jail is no place to be when you have a hostile erection.

No, all this sailor can do is wait out the storm. The issue under the deck has to fix itself at some point, doesn't it? An erection can't last forever, can it? Otherwise, wouldn't the commercials have to say, "Call your doctor if you experience an erection lasting forever"?

In his compromised state, our hero might putter around the garage, careful to avoid injury to his third leg. Or he might lie down in the hammock (on his back, of course). Or he might do some laps in the backyard, grumbling to himself about how he wanted to have more sex with the leaf lady when they were both younger, and when he didn't need these stupid pills—but how she was always tired or something. Or how the carrots weren't being eaten. Or the washing machine was doing whatever.

He still doesn't know what she was talking about back then, because he wasn't actually listening. He was just thinking: *Are you done?* And then: *So, can we do it now?*

AFTER KILLING TIME ALL AFTERNOON and avoiding the gaze of his gossipy neighbors, this trooper would now—finally—be four hours in on the mission and now—finally—with some prescribed cause to call his doctor. This is what he's been waiting to do, and it's really all he *can* do. He's never been the type to ask for help—always a do-it-yourself guy—but duct tape isn't going to solve this problem. Plus, it would hurt like hell.

He knows the drug companies might just say "Call your doctor" because they don't know what to do either. It could be that their scientists saw the potential for phallic catastrophe but still felt the risk was only theoretical, like dark matter or the meat in hot dogs. Or it could be that their lawyers fully realized the liability—indeed, the exposure— of widespread, unabated erections and thus urged a deflective posture: publicly conceding the problem of recalcitrant boners but essentially forcing the medical community to find a solution. For these and other reasons, Woody knows his call to the doctor could be pointless.

But what choice does he have? This thing isn't getting any worse, thank heavens, but nor is it getting any better. All he can really do is dial the number. And wait. And wait some more. And require the clinic to hire more employees to field calls like his. And make the insurance companies raise premiums to cover the increased labor costs. And make the doctor's office schedule more patients into fifteen-minute time slots. And all the other butterfly effects of erectile dysfunction.

The good news is that, with a problem like this, the concerned party would get more attention than boring people calling in with questions about flu symptoms or cancer. Indeed, he would probably even move to the front of the line. Everyone he talks with would almost certainly think: *Wow, I didn't believe that could really happen!*

At first, the receptionist would do that thing where she answers the phone with a "Please hold," giving him no opportunity to contemplate the demand disguised as a greeting.

But when she came back on the line he would concede, "I need to talk to my doctor."

Which would mean she would ask why.

Which would mean he would have to tell her.

Which would mean she would laugh, as she should, before transferring him to the nurse who works with the doctor.

Which would mean he would have to tell her, too.

Which would mean she, too, would laugh, as she should, before paging the doctor.

Which would mean our hero would then have to tell him—or, worse, her—too.

Which would mean he—or, worse, she—would laugh, as he—or, worse, she—should and then say, "I have no idea. Why are you asking me? Try pouring some water on it."

Which is what this poor guy would have to do, because what else *could* he do? His brief session in the leaf pile probably wasn't worth the cost of standing in the backyard with a hose in his pants, but if the doctor's suggestion worked, at least he would finally be on the downside of his uptick. With cold water encouraging normalcy down below, he would find some measure of pride in his war of attrition against the southern hostility. He would feel good about outlasting the uprising. And he would realize that, by returning the feather to his sword, he had somehow become a commanding officer. Indeed, a captain.

THE BURDEN OF PROOF

> Risk homeostasis theory posits that people at any moment of time compare the amount of risk they perceive with their target level of risk and will adjust their behaviour in an attempt to eliminate any discrepancies between the two.
>
> -Gerald J. S. Wilde

DO YOU KNOW HOW MANY KIDS choke every year on that thing you have sitting on your coffee table? You are usually pretty careful, but you set it down this morning when your hands were full and then got distracted. Do you remember that it's there? You will probably put it out of reach very soon, but with the youngster now able to pull himself up and move along the couch, there is a chance *he* might get to it first.

What should you do? Resist taking any action, perhaps to make a point to yourself or others about not being such a worrywart? Go and move it now, so you can begin worrying about something else? Get rid of the coffee table altogether, so you never have this issue again?

These are the kinds of things you might think about as a parent of a young child—or at least as a first-time parent of a young child. American society knows historically low rates of infant mortality, enjoys a greater understanding of nutrition, better isolates environmental toxins, and makes regular improvements in medicine. Yet parents today still seem to worry all the time, even as there should be less to worry about.

Certainly, it's your job to keep kids safe from bona fide dangers, like train tracks and drone strikes, but as you read, research, and realize more than ever before, is your increased awareness of risk worth the constant fretting? Put simply, is it a net gain if you begin to dwell on dangers you never even thought about before you became more aware?

Consider the ways that the recognition of risk and the efforts to minimize it can set you into a feedback loop that has you constantly wondering if there's more you should be doing. These steps are called childproofing, and they are obviously essential at some level; but the word itself might actually be part of the problem. As opposed to the definitive cast enjoyed by this term in a court of law, for example, the "proof" of childproofing isn't really *proof* at all. It's better conceived of in terms of probabilities, proportions, and percentages—better seen as improving the chances of wellbeing while never ensuring it.

Parents take certain measures and hope they will be enough, but lingering doubt often manages to linger on. Which the people who send out catalogs full of baby products seem to know, because when you peruse these offerings under the hold of an anxiety you are still trying to understand, looking over pages filled with instruments, devices, and equipment you didn't even know existed until you went to the mailbox, it can be hard to tell what you really need.

Locks to keep the toilet lid down? Oven knob covers? Thingamajiggers to cushion the corners of the table? Glossy displays of happy, safe, and bruise-free children imply you need all of the above, making it even harder to know when enough is enough: when a decision to buy hints at neurosis and when a decision to forgo indicates neglect.

Sure, you could just refuse all those things you didn't think you needed until the catalogs made you more cognizant, but how would you feel if your toddler went headfirst into one of those uncovered corners of the coffee table? You might want to make a point about overprotective parenting, but is your own kid going to be the canary in that coal mine? Who wants that? If the gizmos are there, and if they offer even one extra degree of safety in the home, how do you *not* make the purchase?

Or is this looking at the problem in the wrong way? Should your true objective be a state of mind that has you not really aspiring toward "proof" at all—accepting, instead, the fact that danger will always be present no matter what you might do? No matter what steps you take.

Even more, what if your efforts to diminish risk actually *increase* it? What if seeking proof encourages a false sense of security, rendering a situation worse than its unprotected prior conditions? What if the extra units of presumptive wellbeing you were stacking up like a protective barrier actually underprepare your kids for the challenges of the world?

A child free to fiddle with childproofed stove controls in the home might be relatively safe within those four walls, but what if he starts doing that in another home, one that has no covers? You might take comfort in the notion that he can't (yet) turn on the stove, but if he doesn't get the underlying message of "Hot! No touch!" is he actually better off in the long run?

Does this mean you should deliberately expose your kids to a hot stove? No, although it wouldn't be surprising to learn that such a school of thought exists somewhere within the parenting universe. It's more a matter of developing a case-by-case and child-by-child sense of judgment as a parent that has you doing what you can to keep your test subject as safe as possible, while also accepting the fact that getting hurt is part of growing up. This, it seems, is the real *burden* of proof.

Danger Ahead

I FELT THIS BURDEN for the first time on the morning we were leaving the hospital with two-day-old Lucas. As I learned, parents with a newborn must receive official permission to leave the grounds, permission that comes from staff members and sometimes ordinary-citizen volunteers who have the power to determine whether your car seat is installed correctly.

These people, car-seat inspectors, are pseudo-agents of the childproofing law for whom "good enough" is never good enough. Car-seat inspectors, for example, don't accept that it's okay for a child-restraint device to be situated somewhere within a range of positions, because they don't recognize the concept of a *range* in the first place. When it comes to safety, there is one—and only one—way to do things.

I wish I had known this ahead of time. Having installed the device, I was careful to follow all the instructions. I tested it for stability several times and deemed it safe and sound. And while I noticed that when the carrier was clicked into its base the arrow on the device did not point to the *exact* middle of the area indicated as acceptable on the side of the unit, I also realized it didn't have to.

Or at least that's what I thought I realized, what I believed to be true, until the ordinary-citizen volunteer scrutinizing our vehicle leaned into the back of the car and shook her head in disbelief. (We'll call her Inspector Ratched, because the allusion to *One Flew Over the Cuckoo's Nest* captures the essence of our relationship.)

With the felt-certainty that flows from faux-authority, Inspector Ratched dressed me down. Here I was, yet another father already failing his young child. I barely had a record as a parent by that point, having only become a dad a matter of hours before then, but I already felt my reputation had been besmirched.

To defend myself, I pulled out the instructions and showed how our arrangement was completely safe: how the manufacturer explicitly said the arrow on the carrier only needed to point somewhere within the two lines on the base for the unit to be at a safe angle relative to the vehicle. The area between these lines was even labeled OKAY.

But Inspector Ratched wouldn't have it, repeatedly insisting that a range of degrees and angles was *always* unacceptable. She didn't go so far as to say the device wouldn't work as I had it set up, but she surely didn't like its design. For her, an arrow could only point to one spot.

I didn't have much with which to counter this contention, having only first thought about car seats the day before, so I promised to buy a new one if we could be on our way. Which we were—but not without a host of new worries. While I had been sure the car seat was safe *before* my interaction with Inspector Ratched, once she got into my head I was only pretty sure. And pretty sure isn't sure enough for a new parent learning to see (and imagine) all sorts of danger ahead.

INSPECTOR RATCHED GOT ME GOING, but my own nervous energy kept me in motion. I had gone from barely tolerating the existence of children to scanning every new setting with threat-detecting eyes. I had become *that* guy—the dorky, obsessive, ridiculous dude watching everyone and everything at every moment of every day. Things really got out of control during my time on family leave, as I was restless, anxious, and in need of something fixed during a period of flux.

Case in point: when Lucas learned to crawl, he was always bumping his head on things, usually because he would be chasing me across the floor and would lose control of his body while rounding corners. He loved playing this game, but there was always a *thud* at some point, then a foreboding second of eerie silence, and then ten minutes of uncontrollable crying.

Since I could not enclose him in bubble wrap, I opted to cover the base of our futon, the legs of the kitchen table, and most of the first two feet of the walls of our living room with the egg-crate foam stuff people place under their bedsheets when they want to pretend they're getting a massage at night. As you can see in this picture, the foam stuff offered at least some amount of protection for Lucas's head.

Sort of, but not really.

Held in place by some nontoxic rope, it worked well for about a month. Until he started trying to walk, of course, wherein he would pull himself up along the futon, clench anything he could for balance, and then fall down with entire foam eggs in both hands. And wherein he would then start trying to *eat* the foam eggs, because, hey, who doesn't like eating foam eggs? Chalk that up as a danger I *created* in my effort to keep him safe.

When it came to protecting Wills, the manifestation of my

childproofing anxiety was a structure we called The Great Wall of Wills. You might just call it an enormous plank of wood secured by two large buckets of concrete, but that's a failure of imagination on your part.

Wills has always been an outside pet, and if it were up to him, he would be outdoors approximately twenty-five hours a day. The problem was, the front of our house was an injury waiting to happen. Descending from the door were five fairly steep stone steps, bounded by ledges about three feet off the ground.

To let Wills be outside, which is where we needed to send him for our own sanity as much as his, we either required a full-time guard stationed at the entrance to Fort Concussion, or we needed some sort of barrier to close off the steps altogether. Since they don't make eight-foot-long baby gates that can be affixed to a rock façade (I looked in all the catalogs), the best I could do was the monstrosity in this photo.

Laugh if you must (seriously, laugh), but it worked.

Sort of, but not really.

It worked for a while, at least, like the egg-crate foam stuff all over the living room. It kept him from getting to the steps—until, of course, he decided that it wouldn't. Until he decided to go over the wall.

Wills had been studying the barrier since day one, actually, casing it like a skillful bank robber, but it wasn't until a few months later that he finally made his move. It's true that he had no real reason to go over the wall—after all, he was already on the fun side, where he wanted to be—but that didn't seem to matter. It wasn't about being on the other side; it was about the wall itself.

For me, the barrier was a precaution; for him, it was a challenge. Like George Mallory heading up Mount Everest, Wills wanted to climb this thing simply because it was there. And when the date of his expedition arrived, or when the random thought of going over the wall fluttered through his head—who knows how decisions are made in that brain—he waited until I went into the garage, put a rock at the base, stepped onto it, and began his ascent.

By the time that I got back to the front of the house, he had crested, gotten himself stuck at the top, and was just hanging there like a towel on the rack. Suspended in mid-air by his then-chubby midsection, and lacking the coordination necessary to shimmy over cleanly, he was a short-term hostage to the device I'd built to protect him.

Unfazed by his predicament, he turned his head toward me, smiled (of course), and said, "Hey Dad, watch dis!" before scooching forward just enough to collapse headfirst onto the steps—onto the steps that had absolutely no egg-crate foam stuff to cushion his fall. Chalk that up as *another* danger I created in my effort to keep a young boy safe.

Off the Leash

THE HOME HAS A PERIMETER, meaning threats can be kept to a somewhat defined area. When kids get beyond that perimeter, however, containment and the management of danger become more challenging. Especially with children like Wills who would toddle off to Sweden if no one was watching.

Because of his innate wanderlust, which he demonstrated from the first day he started walking, we occasionally used a leash to keep him close when we were out in public. Yes, a leash. (I could refer to it as a *harness*, as the daycare did, but it was a leash.) This device allowed him some movement within a radius of three feet in any direction, but it still brought us some peace of mind. It meant we could *grasp* something, a contraption made of reinforced thread from which he could not extricate himself. It assured us that, as long as we held it, it would hold him, meaning he would be near to us—and safe. Of this, we were sure.

Sure, but not settled. You see, using a leash is not a parenting decision that comes easily. Restraining an overly ambitious toddler with one of these things—in an airport, at the carnival, around a body of water—exposes one to looks from strangers that indicate no parent-of-the-year awards are coming any time soon. It's like wearing a sign that says PLEASE JUDGE ME.

When we were out, people would stare—gawk, even—and whisper, "Oh, how could they *do* that to him?" Indeed, sometimes the mortified were so mortified that they took pictures of Wills in his leash, presumably to report on the injustice they had just witnessed.

For all those mothers—and it was always mothers; fathers either laughed or weren't there in the first place—I would ask you this: Do *you* have a kid bent on self-destruction?

And yes, thank you, we know he's a child, not a dog, but they share some tendencies, don't they? Toddlers are also impulsive, also eat food from under the couch, also poop on the floor, and also pant on hot days, right? Why not one more parallel?

As a society, we recognize domains where parents have less than exclusive authority—e.g., kids generally must go to school or its equivalent and there is a line between spankings and state-prohibited child abuse—but there are other domains where decision-making is left to individuals. Like it or not, leash-using is one of those domains; one of those areas where we trust the judgment of mothers and fathers who know their children better than anyone else.

Lucas had not been a leash kid. But Wills definitely was.

NEVER DID I SEE THIS MORE CLEARLY than the time, the *only* time, we went to a certain amusement park in the northeast that seems to specialize in crowds, odors, tattoos, lines, crowds, odors, tattoos, and lines—in that order.

It was hot that day, the place was packed with sweaty people, and the kids were whining, even though the entire day was all about them. Wills was restricted by his leash as we navigated this small city, and the Chorus was outraged. While we walked past a crowd of women from another country (their accents were thick but not discernible), I heard one of them remark, "You see, *this* is what is wrong with American children."

I wanted to engage the commentator a bit, just to hear how wonderful things were where she was from, but I was too self-conscious to respond. I knew it looked bad; but without it, he would run away. The only other options were to put him in a stroller, which he hated, or carry him for five hours, which I hated.

Freedom, agency, and autonomy are all great things in the abstract, but are they great things for a two-year-old? In the abstract, chicken nuggets are great, too, but do you know what's in those things? Who makes decisions in the abstract?

Would it be nice if Wills could walk freely?

Yes.

Would he wander off?

Yes.

How do I know this?

Because he wandered off.

Once we reached a play area, which could also have been called a kids-will-chew-on-rubber-blocks area, we became complacent. There were walls made of netting all around us and only two ways out. We had two parents, one for each exit, and we were prepared to act as border-control agents, willing to stop all children seeking to leave just in case one of them was trying to smuggle out a toddler.

Because it seemed safe and because we were feeling uncharacteristically relaxed in this semi-controlled space, we decided to remove the leash. As I disconnected it, Wills looked around like the suspect does in movies when he realizes the good cop is trying to establish trust by bonding with the arrestee in that psychically intimate way only a good cop can—even as the bad cop fumes in the corner.

Is this for real? his eyes asked, as he shook off the shackles and let the leash fall to the ground in dramatic fashion.

Yes, my son, the stern look in my eyes said in return. *But stay here. In this area. Right here.* I then supplemented those eye-instructions with actual verbal commands, just to be sure.

It's unclear what happened over the course of the next few minutes, but while Lucas and a companion were playing nicely, building some kind of fort with those not-meant-to-be-eaten blocks, Wills escaped.

Can you believe that?

Neither could I.

He was over by Lucas for a bit, helping with the fort, until he was banished for knocking it over. He then moved over to a space where there were not as many kids but where it still seemed fine, because the entire structure was designed for containment. The plateaus for seating made it like an amphitheater, where the kids were on a stage of sorts and where parents could sit above them in an optimal position for observation as the little ones enjoyed the illusion of free rein.

We would occasionally lose sight of Wills as he moved behind bigger kids or crawled under piles of blocks, but we were sure he was somewhere between our respective exits—or at least we were sure of that until Emily yelled to me in a tone and with a look in her eyes recognizable to anyone who has ever thought, if only for a second, that they've lost a child.

"Where *is* he?!" she cried.

My gut sank before she even finished the question.

I looked everywhere, but he was gone.

I took a deep breath and tried to stay calm. This boy is mischievous by nature. I knew he was here, somewhere. He couldn't have gotten by us. There were no escape hatches, this wasn't a James Bond movie, he wasn't Houdini, and he couldn't have spontaneously combusted.

So, where the hell was he?

Five seconds went by, maybe ten. It seemed like years.

If you've been in this awful state of mind, you know the overwhelming surge of emotions. You want to stay under control, but you aren't *in* control. You were in control when he was here, but since he's not here, now *he's* in control. And he has no sense of control—which is the whole point.

I was upset with myself for removing the leash and even more angry at that stupid woman from wherever. This was also *her* fault. Yes, this is what we do in America, but this is also why we do it. We have big, dumb amusement parks, and we try to keep kids from vanishing. I'm sorry if that's too hard for your superior culture to accept.

Are American kids naturally more inclined to escape? Or do they run away because they spend too much time on a leash? These are valid questions to ask; but in that state of mind, I didn't care. I told myself that if I could just find him, I would never take the leash off again. I knew we would never return to this awful place, that's for sure. Nor any other crowded public space. No more chaos. No more people. No more illusion of free rein.

I thought about getting help from a staff member, but I was too embarrassed—which is embarrassing to admit but also true.

No, what I needed to do was stay calm and look around without causing a scene. Wills was small enough to hide between pieces of equipment or station himself behind trash cans. And he might have had accomplices. I wouldn't put it past him to have arranged something in advance, actually. He's that way.

Now it had been about thirty seconds.

Because the netted-in play area was within a sub-domain that was itself segregated from the larger expanse of the amusement park, I decided to go to the access point that let us into this sub-domain and then work my way back toward the last place we had seen him. This way, he couldn't reach the parking lot. Or the water slides. Or Sweden.

Still, there were hundreds of people milling about in this sub-domain. People who could be kidnappers. People who would be blocking my view in selfish pursuit of their own fun. People with whom he might be chatting about the weather. Or jelly beans. Because he's also *that* way.

Taking slow and deliberate steps back to the netted-in play area and being careful not to seem like I was looking for him (because then he would hide for sure), I eventually found Wills a short distance from the point where he had disappeared. As I rushed toward him, I was overcome with relief, sick with shame, bursting with love, and kind of pissed off all at the same time. Since it's hard to know who gets to talk first when anger and elation both want to say something, all I did was hug him and hold him tightly.

He said he'd decided to leave because he was "bored." The rubber blocks didn't taste very good, and he wanted to see the guys throwing balls at bowling pins in another corner of the sub-domain. I was somewhat curious to know how he got by us, two adults who knew (or thought we knew) his potential and proclivities, but I didn't have the strength to ask.

"You were supposed to stay inside the netting," I said, "where we could see you." My voice quivered with the sensation of slowly diminishing panic, but he just smiled (of course), demonstrating what has always been the essence of his nature. It's usually contagious, that spirit and smile of his, but it wasn't so in this moment.

And nor would it be until later that night when he was safe in bed and when I could reflect on how I built a wall to protect him from himself, but he used it as a way to head-butt the steps; how I removed the leash in a leap of faith, but he made me want to cinch it up even tighter; and how I kept pining for the false comfort of proof, but he was continually forcing me to bear its burden.

USE YOUR WORDS

Language is not just a window into human nature but a fistula: an open wound through which our innards are exposed to an infectious world. It's not surprising that we expect people to sheathe their words in politeness and innuendo and other forms of doublespeak.

-Stephen Pinker

LUCAS USED TO STRUGGLE with the letter L, always making it sound like a Y. This was a problem. Not only is L among the more commonly used letters in the English language, it's also the first letter of his name. By kindergarten, he'd learned to make a "tongue sandwich" (where the tongue is wedged between the upper and lower teeth), but his minor speech impediment still caused confusion.

Those who were in regular contact with him, native communicants, understood his tendency to mispronounce certain words. However, those without any context, or those battling background noise, had trouble making sense of him. His furrowed brow indicated *he* knew what he was saying, but they didn't.

When people were stymied in conversations with him, I would occasionally intervene. Like an interpreter at the United Nations, I would offer an explanation of what he was trying to say, why it was hard for him to articulate certain words, and our tongue-sandwich protocol for resolving the matter. Yet there were plenty of times I did not intervene, both because he needed to solve these problems himself and because I found the miscommunication amusing. (I didn't say these were equally good reasons.)

Few things are funnier than kids talking funny. You know this to be true even if you won't admit it. Little ones famously say the "darnedest" things ("She can't have a baby—she's not even married!"). They treat the rules of grammar as mere suggestions ("Me no apple eat!").

And they face issues with enunciation that require parents to hide their laughter behind the open refrigerator door ("More orange douche, please!").

The uninitiated, or those who haven't been in the kid-talk game for a while, find this challenging, often just smiling despite their confusion; but seasoned vets can usually figure out what a child, especially their own child, is saying. Exposure, proximity, repetition, and history give parents the tools of a dragoman, allowing them to manage the misspoken, the omissions, the indiscretions, the disorientation, and the awkward arrangements that befuddle the lay population.

Failure to Communicate

OUR FAMILY HAS EXPERIENCED numerous episodes of kid-centered miscommunication over the years, but none was more memorable than the set of interactions that occurred on a cross-country flight when Lucas was five and Wills was two.

Because he was—and still is—the more wily and unpredictable of the boys, Wills was in the middle seat on this flight, while Emily was at the window and I was on the aisle. This arrangement had Lucas sitting across the aisle, a positioning made possible by his uncanny ability to sit still and concentrate on activities. With a sticker book or video, he'd be good for hours.

It was like traveling with one little kid and one little adult.

On the other side of Lucas, in that row's middle seat, was a grand-mother, perhaps seventy-five years old, with her granddaughter in the window seat. Seeing this woman sitting there had been an immediate relief for us. When you board an airplane with kids, you are always on the lookout for tolerant-seeming fellow passengers—especially older women who, ideally, already have a plate of cookies prepared as they sit there knitting mittens.

By contrast, you do *not* want the obviously single male, usually a businessman, who already has on his Bose noise-killer headphones.

This generally suggests a man who doesn't have kids and doesn't want any reminder that they exist. Such a guy intends to focus only on his PowerPoint slides or the action movie he's downloaded to his new, cutting-edge tablet.

An *older* version of one of these men is a possibility in some cases, since old guys might be grandfathers; but if that's the case, then kids need to be schooled on the comparatively limited range of old-guy-friendly discussion topics. Because grandfathers aren't likely to have any cookies or mittens there to establish rapport, a child who could end up sitting next to one of them needs to be briefed on the things old guys tend to talk about.

"Just ask about the war," I always said to Lucas as we practiced this ritual before boarding.

"Which war?" he would ask, taking the assignment seriously.

"Any war," I would answer. "It doesn't matter—just say *the war* and old guys will take it from there. Old guys always love talking about the war."

"And if that doesn't work," I would add, "try asking if he ever saw Mickey Mantle play. Or if his parents ever lived in a Hooverville. Old guys also love talking about baseball and the Great Depression."

FITTING HER PROFILE WITH EASE, the grandmother on this particular flight was immediately warm and friendly. Peering at Lucas over the top of her glasses, she greeted him with the standard opening line and singsongy voice of a kindergarten teacher, wondering, melodiously, "And what is *your* name?"

As he evaluated this inquiry, Lucas looked over at me for approval. Technically, this woman was a "stranger" and thus generally off limits for verbal engagement. But when I gave him a fatherly nod, he looked back at her, then looked toward his lap, and then said, softly, "Lucas."

Or at least that's what he tried to say—what he meant to say, to be more exact. But it's not quite what she *heard*. Which is why she just smiled and nodded in the way people do when they realize you said something but don't know what it was.

It was an awkward situation. The grandmother clearly wanted to talk with Lucas some more, but they were already at an impasse. She could ask him what his favorite toys were. ("YEGOs," he would say.) And she could inquire of his favorite spotted animals at the zoo. ("Yep-pards," he would tell her.) But what she could not do was ask his *name*. Not again.

That part of their transaction—the introduction, as it were—had already occurred, and the appropriate moment for clarification had passed. The two of them had executed this portion of the deal, at least officially, even though she didn't know what he said and he didn't real-ize she didn't hear him.

Most adults would have sensed some kind of breakdown and prob-ably acted toward a solution, but kids are different. Lucas thought he was done with this conversation and had already returned to his LEGO *Star Wars* sticker book. When Darth Maul had his attention, it was hard to compete—even though, from what I could see, it was clear that his elderly row mate was not done trying to get to know him better.

After a few minutes of interacting with her granddaughter, the grandmother turned back to her left, smiled at Lucas, and waited for him to sense that she wanted to talk some more. I could tell he was ignoring her (a move he learned from me), so I reached over and tapped his shoulder. He looked in my direction, rolled his eyes (another move he learned from me), and then turned toward the grandmother just as she asked, with delight in her voice, "Is your name *Roger*?"

At this, Lucas turned back toward me with a perplexed look on his face. I saw his confusion and raised him one. This was definitely odd. What in the world was she talking about? Why would she be asking if his name is Roger? Hadn't he just told her his name?

About twenty seconds went by with no word from Lucas, but the grandmother was still smiling and still waiting for his response. Not knowing what else to do, he just kept looking at me, wishing he could switch seats with Wills, while I just kept looking at my watch, realizing this flight was now going to be twice as long as normal. The three of us were in the middle of a Mexican standoff, which is hard to execute in horizontal formation on an airplane.

Nothing was said for quite a while. The grandmother and I filled this awkward time by occasionally smiling and nodding back and forth, neither of us quite sure what the other one was doing—or why. But then, after replaying the entire exchange in my mind for several minutes, I finally figured out what was going on. I finally realized that, upon asking his name, what she'd heard from Lucas was not an answer at all—but, instead, an invitation: an invitation to play a game, actually. She thought he was a five-year-old Rumpelstiltskin who had challenged her to *guess* his name.

Which you can see (and hear) if you parse the announced version of his name phonetically—first turning the *L* into a *Y* and then both overemphasizing and overextending the *ooooo* sound of the *U*. Rendering the name in this way affords a seemingly out-of-place pause, somehow allowing an otherwise hard *C* to come across as a totally misbegotten *G*, followed by an impotent *A*, and an *S* at the end that sounds as aggressive as a hissing snake.

For the grandmother, Lucas had not said "Lucas" at all. He had said "Yooooo-gesssss." Or, in other words, "You guess."

"Is it Lawrence?" she continued, unaware that I had just solved the case. "Is it Byron? Is it James?"

Lucas now looked at me with even more visible discomfort. Due to a minor failure to communicate, my painfully shy son was currently the focus of this woman's apparent intention to recite every boy's name she had ever heard. I was starting to think maybe the guy with the Bose noise-killer headphones would have been a much better choice for a row mate, but now it was too late. We judged this book by its cover, and now we had to read it.

Handling Lucas is supposed to be the easy job on an airplane. He behaves himself and remains quiet. We arrange ourselves this way because we need twice the attention on Wills, who fills the time during flights by singing songs, kicking seats, and telling everyone he's the president of Mars.

"Is it Andrew?" the grandmother continued. "Is it Murray? Oh, I know, it's Lester, isn't it?"

Lucas was waiting for me to fix the situation while I was just hoping the captain would interrupt this conversation with an invitation for us all to look out the window at some mountains or a cornfield.

"Wait, is it Roger?" she wanted to know. Again.

Lucas continued to look at me, the grandmother continued to look at Lucas, and I continued to look back and forth between the two of them. Meanwhile, the flight attendant was looking at all of us. She'd come by just to make sure we were wearing our seatbelts.

To be fair, at thirty-five thousand feet, one *does* suffer diminished sensory functioning. Plus, the seating orientation is already ill-suited to conversation, since people aren't arranged in a position where they can easily see facial expressions. And problems are even more likely in interactions between an older person, who is inevitably hard of hearing, and a young boy who has issues with certain . . . "yetters."

Lucas wanted to return to his sticker book, and I was eager to renew our ongoing discussion of the underrepresentation of minority faces in the LEGO minifigure population, but I could see we needed some closure here. The grandmother was unlikely to stumble upon Lucas's actual name—and he was unlikely to try very hard to help her figure things out.

How could we bridge this gap? We didn't need them to have a deep conversation; we just needed him to communicate *one* word. Ideally, we would have had some of those MY NAME IS: _____ stickers you get at mixers. But since we didn't, I just looked right at the grandmother and offered, "He would like to tell you his name."

While her eyes opened wide with glee, Lucas heaved the deep sigh of a five-year-old teenager, turned his head slightly to the right, and proclaimed: "YOOOOO-GESSSSS!"

For reasons already explained, however, this second-effort rendition was unlikely to solve the problem. Lucas was trying to do as he was asked, which he always does, but the effect was to actually make the situation worse. Now it just seemed like he was taunting her.

I wondered how long such a sweet grandmother might keep playing this game. An open-ended contest could take us across America, with increasingly desperate guesses as we headed west. With the low-hanging fruit gone by mid-Pennsylvania, she would be offering up names of cartoon characters by Chicago and would be proposing elements from the periodic table by Omaha.

"Jeremy?" she kept guessing. "Felix? Meriwether?"

Meriwether? I thought. That one was just ridiculous. Actually, most of her guesses were a stretch. She clearly hadn't kept up with popular first names for boys of this generation, two-syllable surnames like Baker, Banker, Booker, Cooker, Rooker, Tinker, and Taylor.

I considered writing down Lucas's name on the cocktail napkin that no one ever uses. I also thought about switching seats with him. I knew that I could easily change the subject, perhaps asking the grandmother whether she'd been in the war, if she'd seen Mickey Mantle play, or if her parents ever lived in a Hooverville. If I didn't do something, she was going to start dredging up references from high-school world-history courses, wondering whether Lucas's name could perhaps be Caravaggio. Or Pontius Pilate.

Deciding to end this once and for all, I again looked right at the grandmother and prepared a tongue sandwich of my own, announcing, as carefully as I could, "His name is Looooo-Cas."

As far as I could tell, this version hit the key vowels and consonants. I spoke the *Looooo* part really well, I must admit, and capped it off with the sort of sharp-edged *C* that we needed to put this matter to rest. She had to understand *me*, right? I'd used my words, and my words are good. None of my language is "yanguage."

The grandmother smiled, I smiled, and Lucas half-smiled. Everything seemed okay . . . until about five minutes later, when I saw her gesturing once again, this time toward me. As I looked toward her with the apprehension of a thirty-something five-year-old, she peered over the top of her glasses and, with a singsongy voice, wondered, melodiously, "And what is *your* name?"

Lost in Translation

CONVERSATIONS WITH KIDS are one thing; conversations *about* them are another. Like politics and religion, children can be a dangerous topic for discussion at dinner parties. For one thing, our kids are an extension of us, meaning things said about them are effectively said about us. But for another, finding out that someone believes in a crazy theory about child development, reads a blog you abhor, belongs to a group urging practices that make you queasy, or refuses to accept the findings of modern science, for example, can threaten or at least complicate relationships between adults.

Sometimes people will confront their differences in order to find common ground, perhaps borrowing tactics from books written to improve communication between adverse parties, such as dogs and cats or Yankees and Red Sox. But for the most part, we tend to sheathe our words in "politeness and innuendo and other forms of doublespeak," as psychologist Stephen Pinker puts it in the epigraph for this chapter. During face-to-face conversations, this means discussants might offer only nonspecific nodding or an occasional "Yeah, I don't know." Those with even basic social skills can usually discern some distance between the two parties and then find ways to shift into topics less controversial, like the weather or contestants on *The Bachelor*.

Alternatively, responses can be delivered in such a way that the listener neither affirms nor denies the speaker's position on the matter, kicking the conversational can down the road. When this is not possible, however—when we can neither redirect nor muddle through with noncommittal "hmmms"—we keep things civil by speaking in code: by employing misdirection, circumlocution, false praise, vagaries, and other techniques of adult-speak that help us work through conversations without really saying anything at all.

Or at least without saying what we *want* to say.

Because there are kids around.

And it sends the wrong message when they see adults in a fistfight.

Conversational challenges can arise between parents and nonparents (who don't speak the language), parents and grandparents (who used to speak the language), and parents and other parents (who may speak a different dialect of the same language). You will see these difficulties demonstrated in the subsections below as you compare what a speaker *says* to what a speaker *means* and to what a listener *thinks* about what has just been said.

While tracking these interactions within the above noted interpersonal domains, you are urged to recognize the doublespeak, smile with approval, and—even if you disagree—muddle through with noncommittal "hmmms." This is how big people use their words.

nonparents

NONPARENTS LIVE IN A DIFFERENT WORLD. As a result, it can be very difficult to talk with them, especially those who are happily nonparental. Conversations with the childless may not be fraught with tension, as they can be between one parent and another, but this is because nonbreeders have no skin in the game.

And also, they really don't give a shit what you're talking about.

They don't care about this theory of sleep training or that school of thought on allergies; they think only of the new brunch spot they'll visit on Sunday morning and the fancy convertible they just bought with no room at all for a car seat. They go on vacations that are actually fun, and they see movies that are still in the theaters. These kinds of people don't want to hear about your kid, see his picture, talk with him, or even talk with you if you're going to talk about him.

New parents, those who have recently crossed over from the non-parent world, often forget from whence they came and assume their ramblings make sense to the uninitiated.

But they don't.

As an example, new parents insist on phrasing a child's time on this planet in terms of "months" rather than years. I remember this well, because I thought it was so stupid—that is, until I had a young child and realized it makes perfect sense.

You have been in this conversation before, on one side or the other, so you know how it goes. A nonparent notices you have a blanketed bundle and decides out of courtesy to express some slight interest in the creature. This usually takes the form of a seemingly straightforward question such as: "How old is it?"

Having been a vigorous partisan on that side of the matter, I know that a nonparent just wants a nice and easy whole-number response.

But it doesn't work that way.

The kid-wise out there understand that, for babies and young toddlers, new stuff is happening every month, every week, and every day. According to especially excited first-time parents, new stuff is even happening every minute. Just look on Facebook.

Parent/Nonparent Translation

PARENT *SAYS*	PARENT *MEANS*	NONPARENT *THINKS*
"Six days ago, he turned fourteen and a half months old. They grow up so fast!"	My child is almost fifteen months old, but we can't yet claim that step, because it would violate the parental-milestones code of conduct.	*Huh? He just turned fourteen and a half months old? What? Just say he's one, okay? Or ten. What's the difference? I'm a nonparent for a reason. They all look the same to me, anyhow.*

grandparents

SOMETIMES PEOPLE ARE technically "parents" but not in the manner relevant to this discussion. These individuals have children, yet it's been a long time since they got up with a baby at one o'clock in the morning or helped someone with homework. When parents get older like this, detached from the day-to-day matters of tending to little kids—and when their own kids finally have some kids—they morph into something called grandparents.

Grandparents are tricky, because while they *did* raise a child (you, for example), that was back when everything was easier. They may not think it was easier, but it had to be. How could it have been any harder? Grandparents sometimes only vaguely recall their child-rearing days, but they definitely remember what kind of liquor helps soothe toothaches. And they also know when children need a firm swat to the butt, just like their preacher used to deliver after church.

Because of this experience, filtered through aging brain cells, grandparents often have strong views on how you should be raising your child. For example, elders are dubious of numerous practices of Generation X and millennial parents, such as taking kids to the doctor even when they are "well," applying hand sanitizer before touching the hand sanitizer dispenser, and, of course, pumping, bagging, labeling, freezing, thawing, warming (but never microwaving), and then bottling breast milk.

Grand*fathers*, in particular, can't get over the very name of that thing—a breast pump—shaking their heads in disbelief with each utterance. Back in the war, no one talked about breast pumps. Meanwhile, grand*mothers* wonder why you can't just buy the powdered stuff they sell at Costco. Grandmothers love Costco. They also love pushing breast milk research right back at you with a look that says: *I didn't do all that stuff, and you turned out fine.*

You would like to tell a grandmother that, to be honest, you are *not* fine—but then she would be miffed. And you need her to babysit this weekend. Thus, the safest approach is to simply sheathe your words in politeness, innuendo, and forms of doublespeak, before moving on to discuss the highlights of the new ad circular that just came in the mail from Costco.

Grandparent/Parent Translation

GRANDPARENT *SAYS*	GRANDPARENT *MEANS*	PARENT *THINKS*
"Now is it all nuts, all legumes, all dairy products, and all fruits that start with a P that he can't have? What else should we avoid this weekend? Is it okay if the organic farmers wore non-latex gloves when they picked the berries? I mean, as long as they have been paid a fair wage? We just want to respect your wishes."	You realize this is all bullshit, right? How come, all of a sudden, an entire generation is allergic to the foods that made America great? You were probably "allergic," too, but we didn't call it that, and you were eventually exposed in doses that gave you some immunity—which is what you *should* be doing with our grandchild. Your generation is loony, and you'd see that if you pulled your faces away from screens once in a while.	*Back off, Mom and Dad. I'm stressed out with work right now, and I don't have time to sort the wheat from the chaff. (By the way, he's also allergic to chaff.) Just keep the EpiPen with you. Your generation taught us about hot things by throwing us into camp-fires. Get off your high horse before you fall and break a hip.*

other parents

TALKING WITH OTHER PARENTS is easier in some ways, harder in others. Proximity allows for higher-level talks, because you're both in the know; although, in certain cases, this familiarity can push the parties toward even more cryptic postures. In communication between parents in the *same* family, this tends to take the form of statements routed through a third party, typically the child.

This turns the little one into a transmitter of passive-aggression, as in the case of comments such as: "Why doesn't your father ever put this pan away?"—which a mother might say to a baby in a high chair even though the father is sitting at a table five feet away. In a few years, a snappy toddler will be able to offer some conjecture ("Is it because Daddy is *dumb?*"); but until then, the youngster is just there to capture impressions and file them away to the deep stacks of the subconscious.

Beyond the household, where the parties are both parents—yet are neither married nor united in any meaningful way—conversations take a different form. For example, say two kids bonk heads while collecting both bacteria and viruses as they roll around in a McDonald's Play-Place. One parent sees the contact, rushes over, soothes his own flesh and blood, and assigns blame to the other child—a verdict made easier to render due to the fact that the other child's mother is too busy texting and stealing her son's fries to even realize he's been detained.

With a slight glance at the offending child, the intervening parent offers comfort to his own precious little one, reiterating the importance of playing nicely, being careful, taking turns, and other things Robert Fulghum learned in kindergarten—even though the lecture is actually only directed at the other child, the bad one. The intervening parent's child, the good one, already knows all that stuff. Because he's perfect.

An indirect scold of this sort allows the intervening parent to shame the other child—again, the bad one—and also the offender's derelict, text-addled, and fry-stealing mom, without escalating the situation. Which is important in inter-parent disciplinary disputes, since the incident is still officially outside the intervening parent's jurisdiction. Beyond the above suggested scold, all the intervening parent can really do is emit disapproving parental energy into the atmosphere while fixing judgmental looks upon the other child—once more, the bad one—for an hour or so.

Or maybe two.

Three at the most.

As a matter of principle, the intervening parent cannot consider this case closed until the evil lad shows at least some small measure of contrition, maybe giving up the kind of toothless apology-as-non-apology that politicians offer when they say "mistakes were made." Or perhaps washing away the entire affair with one of those vague concessions big corporations grant when they settle lawsuits charging them with killing people and then issue a statement saying they plan to "move forward" and "begin a new day" in order to, most likely, resume killing people.

Parent/Other Parent Translation

PARENT *SAYS*	PARENT *MEANS*	OTHER PARENT *THINKS*
"No, no, Susie, that's not ours. That's Johnny's race car. Don't touch, sweetie! I know it looks fun, just sitting there with no one playing with it for the entire play date, but it's not ours."	Bitch, will you just let Susie play with the damn thing?! I'm tired of talking in this saccharine voice while struggling to reconcile the preschool value of *sharing* with the social contract concept of *property*. Your awful little Johnny only wants the car because Susie wants it, and you know it. What a brat.	*Oh, really, Susie's mom? You want me to let your little diva play with this toy? Why? Just because you can't discipline her? Because you give her whatever she wants just to avert a tantrum? No, Susie's mom, no. Not today. Today, I'm Charlton Heston, and you'll only get this race car by seizing it from my cold, dead hands.*

IN THE END, adult-speak can be as hard to understand as kid-talk. Something is said; something else is heard. Something is intended; something else is perceived. Something is implied; something else is inferred.

We say "use your words," but it's never that simple.

Even for adults. Actually, especially for adults.

Well, not all adults, I guess. The guy in the Bose noise-killer headphones has it all figured out. Just ask him.

THE CHILDREN'S MENU

What?! I have to eat *all of it*? How much is that?

-Wills

T HE EMPLOYEES CAN SEE YOU coming from a distance. They always notice when a family car is circling the parking lot. They know what it means when bumper stickers broadcast honors attained in preschool. They are able to hear children's songs playing inside the vehicle. They can tell that parents have arrived. And, even worse, they've brought children with them.

Parents know what this means, too, even if they've conveniently forgotten everything learned the last time they considered going out to eat with their kids. If they've chosen a kid-oriented establishment— where, for example, adult meals *also* come with crayons and ice cream—the staff members are usually resentful of their current employment situation. As a matter of professional necessity, servers will be familiar with typical parental requests (e.g., "Will you put a rush on that pizza?" and "Can we have more of this yellowish stuff you said was juice?"); but even if they are competent in this milieu, they aren't content. They want out of this land of teenage busboys, menus the size of novellas, and cooks addicted to crystal meth.

The situation isn't much better at one of those generic chain restaurants where the employees' vests are so full of flair you can't discern the color of the underlying fabric. Menu options in these kinds of establishments might be slightly more appealing for adults, but this still won't be a pleasant dining experience. Parents will order some food, have high hopes for a good meal, and attempt some conversation—but then they will end up regretting they went out, have their food boxed up, and (once again) resolve to just stay home next time.

I have been on both sides of this line, first working the obligatory stints in chain restaurants as a young adult and now frequenting such venues with my family. I know how people talk in the kitchen. I know what goes on at the hostess booth, behind the bar, and out back where the servers are all puffing away on cigarettes and complaining about having to deal with bratty kids. I know firsthand how busboys loosen the tops of saltshakers at the tables of servers who are being especially bitchy that evening. I know about the unwritten policy of banishing families to the restaurant's equivalent of Siberia. And I know you should not go out to eat with your children until they are at least twenty-five.

IT GOES ABOUT THE SAME every time we go. We get out of the car, walk through the parking lot while dodging two-ton missiles, and are greeted at the door by a perky hostess who says she is "*soooooooo* happy" we decided to join them for dinner. (We'll call her Brittany, because most of them are named Brittany.)

I always tell Brittany that we are just as happy as she is, but Brittany never hears my response, because Brittany only does greetings, not dialogue. Still, she is darn good at hostessing and, within seconds, is already in front of the dry-erase board studying the evening's server-section cartography. This usually includes a few tables being crossed out, some ad hoc annotations (e.g., 86 FISH and NEW DESSERT YUCKY!), and also the pager number for the assistant manager, even though he's rarely more than ten feet away from anyone, especially the younger women employees. (We'll call him Randy, because most of them are named Randy.)

Brittany looks frustrated, and I know what she's going through right now. It's difficult being in charge of the server rotation. Politics pervades social relations under this roof, as anywhere, and the drama can make for unforgiving implications—particularly on a night like this with big decisions to be made.

Brittany already realizes she's going to make one server very upset this evening. (We'll call her April, because many of them are named April.) Brittany knows it's April's turn to get a table; but at the same time, Randy's personal policy for weekend nights is to send *all* parties with kids to the section of the restaurant obscured by the big plastic tree. And that entire section belongs to another server. (We'll call her Autumn, because the ones not named April are named Autumn.)

The problem is, Autumn just got a table; another family, in fact. You might think Autumn would like that—having more business, making more money—but she doesn't. She's kind of lazy. Thus, Brittany can opt to please Randy, but piss off April *and* Autumn; or she can please April, but earn a rebuke from Randy and probably a look of feigned outrage from Autumn.

Such a decision tree requires Brittany to go out on a limb—but which one? She knows April could surely handle a family. Those types can be annoying, but April's got a good fake smile and has managed them before. Plus, her only customer right now is the elderly guy at table seventeen who came in at four o'clock in the afternoon with his laminated tip-calculation sheet. Since he's been working out the gratuity on his three-dollar check for about twenty minutes now, April has some time on her hands before the dinner rush begins.

Still, Randy wants to keep his best server in the main section of the restaurant, where real people will be attempting to enjoy their meals as far from children as possible. Thus, he's explicitly barred April from crossing jurisdictional lines by taking any tables in Siberia, the land of the big plastic tree. It just gets too complicated for the employees doing "Expo" (industry jargon for the people who bring out your food and who usually look confused because they're usually very, very high).

As Brittany sees it, the only solution is to double-seat Autumn. Doing so will virtually guarantee angry looks coming in from April all night, particularly as April stands at the silverware-folding station and gossips with other servers, but this is where Brittany makes her money.

At least *Randy* will be pleased, so she'll get some better hours next week.

Feeling the courage of this newfound conviction, Brittany looks up at us, grabs some crayons and children's menus, and asks, "Will we be needing a high chair this evening?"

When Brittany—this Brittany, any Brittany—asks the question in this way, I like to respond by saying, "Do *we* need one? No, we don't need one—but if *you* want one, that's fine."

Sadly though, there is not a single Brittany at any hostess booth I've ever encountered who has gotten that joke. Or maybe they did get the joke but just thought I was an asshole. Either way, after an uncomfortable few seconds with insincere smiles going both ways, Brittany takes us to our table, wishes us a pleasant meal, and exits the scene.

This is always the point at which our children declare they are "starving" and ask how long it will be until the food arrives. "Shush," I say, whenever they do this, which is every time. "You will do the kid activities on the menu, coloring this and that and occupying yourself in some way while I talk to Mom."

The crayons they've just been given are the cheap kind that break whenever you look at them, and the children's menu has the usual crossword puzzles with the restaurant's offerings as the answers, as well as some skeletal diagrams of chickens eating hamburgers and vice versa. Those things all need to be colored in and then ripped to shreds. Which the boys do, at least for a minute or so, until Lucas, the young Frank Lloyd Wright, begins building a house with sugar packets, just as Wills, the game show host, starts chatting up people walking by and wondering aloud whether anyone wants to hear him fart.

After a delay that is longer than you would expect for a server with only one other table, Autumn approaches, leading with her very best *I really like kids* face and trying hard to engage the little ones.

But with no luck. They just stare at her, utterly transfixed by all her flair. It's up and down her vest, with some even hanging down her back and below her waist, making it look like she has a tail. Her name badge indicates she's been part of the "team" for about a year now, which I take to be a good sign. It means she will know how to do things—or at least it should mean that.

Autumn suggests we start with drinks, which is always a good idea. I toy with the prospect of a Long Island Iced Tea but decide the evening does not yet call for such high-dose medicine. Instead, I opt for a draft beer. It seems so simple: you just need someone to pull a tap and, of course, someone to inform you of the current selections.

This is where Autumn comes in. The list on the wall by the bar doesn't help those of us stationed on this side of the big plastic tree, because there are no binoculars at the table. Having been to this restaurant before, I know there are certain options that are always available, but I also know they occasionally add a different one so they can claim their beers are "always changing in new and exciting ways."

"*Autumn*," I say, with an inflection indicating I'm counting on her expertise, "could you tell me what you have on tap tonight?"

Despite the considerable tenure advertised on her badge, the beer list is always a challenge for Autumn. Every single Autumn. And every single time we come in, in fact. Which is really hard to believe when you do the math. If we assume that Autumn works two or three nights per week, and that she walks by the bar one hundred times per night, then we know she has seen the levers on the taps, the large beer menu by the bar, and the reminder sheets on the wall about thirteen thousand times in the last year.

"Um," Autumn begins, sounding her characteristic hesitation and initiating the ritual whereby we both crane our necks and work together to read the taps over the horizon of the bar seventy-five feet away. "Hmmm . . . well," she continues, squinting as best she can, "it looks like one of them is called Bud-something."

Surprised to hear that an obscure beer like Budweiser would have a presence in a national chain restaurant, I perk up.

"Great!" I say, acting excited about enjoying a bland American lager. "And are there any others?" I inquire, raising my eyebrows to signify a conversational handoff.

She nods and reads off one called Coors. But then we both have to wait until the bartender gets out of the way so we can see the rotating billboard listing the two "seasonal" offerings.

Once that happens, Autumn tells me that one of them is named Miller, which doesn't really strike me as a seasonal beer, while I can see that the other one is called Blue Tail Ale, even though Autumn thinks it says Blue *Tall* Ale.

"So, you have a total of *four* beers on tap?" I ask, using my fingers for effect but still finding it hard to believe this could be the universe of options for a chain with "amazing locations" across America.

"Yeah, I guess," Autumn says, looking bored of me already. "There used to be only three, but then Randy added the one called Bud or whatever, because he says people love beer from Milwaukee."

I consider correcting her—or him, actually—but realize there's no point. Instead, I say, "Autumn," with a look bestowing the compliment that she must surely be of age, "have you tried the Blue one—the one that is either a Tail or a Tall?"

"Well," she confesses, "actually, I don't even *like* beer."

This is truly shocking. How is Autumn going to pad the bill with expensive alcohol add-ons using a soft-sell approach that's so soft it's mushy? Our dining experience is quickly going to hell, and we haven't even placed food orders yet.

"But," she follows up, showing me a hint of Dale Carnegie, "like, um, my friend had it the other night, and she said it was super yummy."

Since I have a personal rule against using the word *yummy* to describe beer, I decide to make a hard pivot.

"Autumn," I announce, in a tone indicating that now the evening *does* call for such high-dose medicine, "I have instead decided to have a Long Island Iced Tea. Can you bring me one of those?"

"But that's not one of the four—" Autumn starts to respond, leading me right to her rescue.

"Yes, I know, Autumn. It's not a beer. It's a mixed drink. You do have a bar over there, right? Isn't that where the bartender is standing? And isn't that bar functional? And isn't it stocked with bottles of liquor? What I would like is for your bartender to pour from those bottles and create for me a very, very strong Long Island Iced Tea."

"Um, okay," Autumn says, still sounding unsure about the new plan. "Long Island Tea."

"No, no," I rush in, seeing where this could go. "Long Island *Iced* Tea."

Then I give her a look that asks: *Can we get that started?* (industry jargon for putting in an order).

"Er, right," she murmurs. "So, did you want that sweetened or unsweetened?"

BY THIS POINT, Emily has had it with my alcohol-focused information-gathering efforts and begins to pursue the putatively more important objective of getting food to our poor children as soon as possible. Which shouldn't be too hard to accomplish, because the boys are quite eager to order from this menu—loaded as it is with starchy, salty, fried, breaded, cheesy, meaty, greasy, and oily options, plus a few side dishes that probably won't even be touched.

After carefully searching for the least healthy choices, Lucas opts for the fried fritter franks as his main course, with "mixed vegetables" that are mostly corn as his preferred side, while Wills agrees in principle to the strips of breading with chicken, served with three mandarin orange slices straight from the can. Each meal is a true bargain at twelve dollars, especially considering the "free" dessert.

Emily and I put in orders for this and that, fully realizing that if our own meals look at all enticing the barbarians will be at the gates demanding to have some. As a deterrent, I sometimes request that my entrée be enclosed by a wall of parsley, knowing from experience that the boys will be repulsed by a leafy green barrier. They both dislike green things. One of them also doesn't like yellow things. The other has occasional opposition to red things.

Autumn tells us she will "get those going right away" (industry jargon for getting things going right away), and somehow the kids' food is delivered before she even leaves the table. This is good, because it means the whining will stop for a minute; but it's also bad, because it means the parent/kid dinners are not synchronized. The kids will be done and clamoring to leave before the adults have even eaten.

The youngsters devour the preferred elements of their meals, before briefly picking over their sides and then declaring themselves "full." They insist they cannot eat another morsel, meaning the orange clumps and corn matter that count as their nutrients will likely be returned to the earth. Or perhaps to a factory somewhere to be processed into batches of Soylent Green.

When this happens, I threaten to locate a shovel and then cram food into their mouths like fathers used to do in television sitcoms. Emily, however, takes a softer approach, helping the boys to see that if they'll just ingest these small bits of mostly edible material, they'll be able to get a delicious dessert that will end up neutralizing the nutrition that punched its ticket. This helps the lads realize they actually *aren't* full, especially as a bowl of chocolate decadence is presented to another boy a few tables closer to the big plastic tree. That kid had previously been quite loud but then turned eerily silent as the pile of sugar was given to him.

"Whoa, can we get *that?*" our children ask, as drool begins pooling on the table.

I choose not to answer them, hoping they will forget they have asked a question, as they often do. But my approach here, a style of parenting I refer to as the Just Ignore Them Method, is complicated by Autumn's eventual return to the table.

Reeking of Kool Menthols and showing even more false enthusiasm than usual, she asks, "Is everything cooked just right?" (industry jargon for "I don't really care one way or the other") and seems genuinely surprised to learn that the adults at the table never actually received their meals. Promising to "get right on that" (industry jargon for getting someone else to do it), she then wonders whether the kids are ready for their free desserts.

Moving my chair just a bit to see around the big plastic tree, I can read a sign near the back of the house (industry jargon for the kitchen) that states kids' meals are only supposed to come with a popsicle or a bag of animal crackers. I know those options won't suffice now that the chocoholics have seen what else is out there, so I gesture toward the other boy's table, where he now has his entire head inside the bowl, and ask if we can get two of those.

This request makes Autumn visibly distressed, because that concoction, Sundae Bloody Sundae, is one of the restaurant's *premium* options and is never supposed to count as a free dessert. Nonetheless, Autumn obliges, seeks Randy for permission to key in a special item, and suffers his leering as he stands uncomfortably close and wonders what she's doing after work.

Within a minute, the desserts are delivered to the table by an Expo runner so high he doesn't even realize he's licking whipped cream off his fingers all the way from the kitchen. Undeterred by this sanitary infraction, the children begin ingesting their caloric debacles with such intensity that they stop breathing for long stretches of time.

This is when Randy comes by the table to inquire about the service. And upon hearing that Autumn never managed to facilitate anything other than the kids' meals, including that medicinal and much-needed Long Island Iced Tea, this is also when he seems most embarrassed to be alive. As Randy explains it, Autumn failed the menu exam over ten times and still gets overwhelmed when trying to process orders for adults. She would prefer to simply greet people at the table, work with them to read from the beer listings on the other side of the restaurant, and magically ensure all children's menu items are delivered right away.

Leaving for only a matter of seconds, Randy returns with some food for the big people at the table—not what we ordered, but whatever— just as Autumn brings us the bill. And just as she explains, in her most sincere voice, "I'm *totally* not trying to rush you or anything" (industry jargon for "Hurry the hell up—my shift is ending soon!").

We get our meals boxed up, leave a solid tip for Autumn (I mean, come on, she still has to pay her rent, right?), earmark a few dollars in cash for the busboy who will have to deal with the compost pile underneath the table, and make our way to the door.

As we pass the hostess booth, Randy stops flirting with Brittany long enough to say, "Come back again real soon, y'all." Which is nice, to be sure, even if it does seem forced. Randy had neither a southern accent nor a rural affect when we first arrived—or even five minutes before, when he was standing at our table explaining why Autumn thinks her job is too hard.

I assume he's overdoing the hospitality on our way out so that we will once again forget about our experience and return as customers. He realizes this wasn't Autumn's best performance, and he also knows Budweiser is actually made in Cleveland not Milwaukee, but he's given up trying to teach Autumn about beer. It's too much for her.

If Autumn is ever your server, just order from the children's menu. Maybe get yourself a nice strawberry lemonade. It's super yummy.

MUST SEE TV

Oh, no—absolutely not. We definitely haven't seen that program. In fact, we don't even *own* a television. We don't believe in them. Our little Siegfried just meditates for relaxation.

-that annoying parent

T ELEVISION ALWAYS SEEMS to get a bad rap. Criticism comes from parenting guides, social media, librarians, and daytime television programs that have, without acknowledged irony, booked guests to discuss the evils of television. Shame even comes from little critters called Oompa-Loompas. I'm sure you remember them: they were central figures in Roald Dahl's book (later to become a movie, twice) *Charlie and the Chocolate Factory*.

The Oompa-Loompas played various roles in this story, but one of their jobs was to chant a new lesson each time a bratty child would succumb to his or her signature vice. One of those bratty children was Mike Teavee, a boy obsessed with television westerns. As readers (and viewers) learned, poor Mike was so impulsive that he basically ended up being broadcast by the very medium of his weakness—whereupon, the Oompa-Loompas arrived on the scene, adopted their usual hectoring tone, and chastised parents of this earlier generation for allowing kids to stare at the television until they had become hypnotized by its transmissions.

Perhaps such a critique was justified at the time. Back in the early 1960s, when Dahl began churning out trippy novels for children, maybe it *was* true that staring at a television would rot your brain. Viewing options were basically limited to a baseball game or two, *The Ed Sullivan Show*, *Gunsmoke*, and *The Huntley-Brinkley Report*. There was, as of yet, no *Sesame Street*, no Disney Channel, and probably not even any reruns of

Law & Order. There was just a big box that sat in the living room and fascinated everyone—a big box that kept kids from reading books about truly wholesome activities, like eating a bunch of candy while touring a factory with a madman.

For Dahl, the Oompa-Loompas were spokesmen—strange, creepy-looking little spokesmen—for a campaign of resistance. They offered an absolutist approach based on fear of the unknown. Television was a relatively new thing back then, eliciting the same kind of apprehension people initially felt when radio technology was first introduced, or when books themselves became more available to the masses. In essence, Mike Teavee was a representation of the vanity and all-consuming prospects of the medium: a caricature used to chastise parents for relying on this newfangled device as a babysitter.

It's a reasonable concern, but the response was surely overblown. Teetotaling rarely works. As a society, we do better with limits and moderation. The discretion of *occasional* is much preferred, implying that even less-than-optimal activities can be acceptable in small doses. Sure, watching television—and being on "screens," in general—can go too far, but anything can go too far.

The tube is no replacement for creative or physical activities, such as reading, coloring, and climbing trees, but watching some programming doesn't rot your brain. And staring at the screen, like when the favored team is marching down the field, or when the HBO series is in the last few minutes of the season finale, isn't being checked out. It's being locked in. There's a difference.

WITH EMILY GONE BEFORE DAWN nearly every weekday, mornings have always been challenging for me. When it was only Lucas who I needed to get ready for daycare, it was hard enough; but with two kids, I regularly relied on the assistance of television or television programs broadcast through other devices. Few things work better when you need to clean up the dishes, get ready for work, or redirect wayward children who have once again gotten up at five-thirty in the morning, despite an expressed prohibition against ever waking up that early. For any reason. Ever.

I rationalized these television and general screen-time privileges by finding ways to make the boys watch with more intention than they otherwise would. Specifically, I assigned them to analyze the shows they were viewing, just as I always required the college students in my classes to carefully scrutinize videos that supplemented our course readings. Kids—younger people in general, but especially little kids—are often visual learners, and thus thirty minutes of the Disney Channel has the potential to serve as a genuine educational opportunity. Adults need not jointly view the shows their children are watching in the other room, since that would defeat the purpose of distracting them with this activity in the first place; but a grown-up, the teacher in this regard, should be familiar enough with the programs to ask tough questions that will get kids to evaluate what they've just seen.

In this way, viewing is not a wholly passive activity. Little ones get to watch something for a while but must then belly up to the kitchen table to begin the process of meaning-making. This refines a child's analytical abilities, develops his critical-thinking skills, and even encourages *self*-imposed limits on his viewing—because, seriously, what kid wants to sit down for a seminar discussion of a cartoon?

You see? Everyone wins.

As a public service to the busy parents of the world, I have provided below ten questions that can be used to get you through the same rough mornings. And afternoons. And evenings. Feel free to modify these prompts to suit your own child's needs, strengths, or weaknesses. If he leans heavily toward cartoons, explore the parallels between the animated and actual worlds. If he has moved on to sitcom-style shows, with tweens as main characters and annoying laugh tracks, press him on why they need to provide their own laughter if the show is supposed to be funny. And if he often seems amused by the misfortune of others (e.g., anvils dropped on heads or superheroes killed by meteors), have him checked out by a professional. It's best for everyone if we spot psychopaths at an early age.

Discussion Questions

1. Compare and contrast the guys from *Imagination Movers* and *The Wiggles*. Avoid facile similarities (both involve outfits, both involve four adult men jumping around looking ridiculous). Pay special attention to the claim that the Imagination Movers are really just "Imitation" Movers: a poor man's group of Wiggles in virtually every respect. Is the "movers" shtick just an effort to present these guys as proletarian as opposed to the bourgeois Wiggles? Is this why the Movers wear jumpsuits? Why would a grown man wear a jumpsuit? For that matter, why does the main Mover always have goggles resting on his head? What do goggles have to do with loading furniture on a truck?

2. Is it appropriate for adults to blurt out answers to the questions posed by Mickey in *Mickey Mouse Clubhouse*? Mickey tends to throw some soft pitches that make it hard not to take a swing. For example, he will ask the audience what item he should use to play some golf, before giving viewers the following options: (a) a chainsaw; (b) a watermelon; (c) a golf club; and (d) a cheetah. If an adult gets the answer before a toddler has even heard the question, is he teaching an important lesson about being forthright? Or is he just being kind of a dick?

3. Explicate the meaning of *exploration* as this concept is experienced by Dora and her band of speaking animals and instruments in the program *Dora the Explorer*. Pay particular attention to the following question: Can one really be an "explorer" while carrying a talking map and without ever leaving the well-marked path

through the forest that has no more than three or four trees? If you have a backpack that would make MacGyver jealous, and if you always walk safely past the crabs and crocodiles of the Mexican countryside on your way up Strawberry Mountain, do you really deserve the same job title as Christopher Columbus?

4. Dora is a cousin of Diego. Both kids reign over television empires, with ample cross-fertilization. Your question is this: Which of the cousins is the bigger draw? Who has more sway in the hallways over at Nickelodeon? This query requires you to poll your playmates. Be sure to control for key characteristics as you conduct the survey (don't ask only boys, don't ask only maps, don't ask panthers at all). Dora has seniority, but don't forget that marketers love the four-year-old-male demographic.

5. What's going on in *Tom and Jerry*? In the show, Jerry is a mouse, traditionally considered a pest and generally unwelcome in the home. Meanwhile, Tom is a cat, traditionally considered a house pet and often given the keys to the castle. Why then do viewers seem to view Jerry as the hero? Explain.

6. In *Arthur*, the main character is an aardvark. Most people don't know this. By contrast, Arthur's best friend, Buster, is unequivocally a rabbit. Buster has floppy ears and big front teeth. Your question is this: Is *Arthur* a more compelling cartoon because no one has any idea what Arthur is while they're watching the show? If the main character was a donkey or an elephant—or even if the show was all about Buster—would you be less likely to watch because you'd feel like you already have a handle on the lives of donkeys, elephants, and rabbits? Does the ambiguity in *Arthur* cause you to judge the main critter more by the content of his character than the color of his fur?

7. Try and recall a show called *Teletubbies*. I only let you watch it one time, and that was mostly for my own amusement. One of the characters was named Tinky Winky. Do you remember him? Did anything seem wrong with him, other than being a Teletubby? Some adults think Tinky Winky presents a serious threat to children, because he might be trying to lure them into lives of Tinky-Winkyness. I want to know what you think. Does seeing Tinky Winky make *you* want to dress in purple, wear a triangle hat, carry a purse, hop around the hills of England, and develop an interest in other Tubbies of the same Tele-sex?

8. In *Curious George*, George is described as "curious." Based on the episodes you've seen, what does that word mean in this context? George is always smiling, so why isn't the show called *Happy George*? He gets along great with his friend who lives out in the country—the one who calls him "kid" for some reason—so why isn't the show known as *Friendly George*? George only mildly torments the dog that lives in the lobby of his apartment building— the one always fastidiously cleaning up everything due to a case of canine OCD—so why isn't the program titled *Empathetic George*? Or even *Mischievous George*, since he always clogs up pipes with his toys and swallows puzzle pieces?

9. Please explain to me the appeal of *Thomas & Friends*. I don't get it. It's so boring that I fell asleep three times just writing this question. Thomas is not animated, he doesn't blow anything up, he doesn't talk to animals, he doesn't speak Spanish, and he neither sings nor dances. The plot for each episode is about as bland as English cooking. A fat little man runs the operation on the island—and, while he isn't ruthless, he toys, if you will, with the emotions of some of the more fragile engines in the gang, lauding a few for being "really reliable" but chastising others who are

only a minute late, even if it was the fault of the Troublesome Trucks. How is this interesting for an age group that supposedly needs the stimulation of flashes, bangs, and booms? I pay attention because I like hearing George Carlin's narration, but why do you watch this show?

10. *Handy Manny* is a program about a guy who is certainly handy, but some might say the show toils in ethnic stereotypes. Manny is a hard-working guy who does a great job helping out the principal, a man who cannot even change a light bulb, and he contributes in all sorts of positive ways to the community. But he's also marked by his heavily accented English. A sophisticated viewer can infer that Manny came from south of the border, which is fine, but what we don't know is why his tools *also* speak heavily accented English. If he brought them from his home country, that's one thing; but if he just got them from Home Depot after crossing over, then this doesn't make any sense. Tools don't pick up an accent just because their new owner talks that way. More important is the fact that Manny, the only Hispanic adult-male lead character in a cartoon broadcast in America (I think), is basically a day laborer. I get that "Handy" plus "Manny" is a play on "handyman," but the creators of the show could have given Manny the same first name while having him work, instead, as an orthopedic surgeon, right? Surgeons who rebuild wrists are also handy, aren't they? Do you kids have any idea what I'm talking about?

SUBMISSION: All responses are due by naptime. Answers must be three sentences in length. No, you may not write the same sentence three times. Yes, you may be considered exempt from this assignment if you agree to take a longer nap. Or two.

OEDIPUS WRECKS

Researchers have shown that the particular way fathers play
with their children makes their kids more curious and im-
proves their ability to learn.

-Louann Brizendine

W HILE THE WORDS *paternal* and *parental* have much in common,
they certainly aren't synonyms. A man might act in a paternal
way but still not necessarily be a parent, as a father-figure, for example.
And a man might technically be considered a parent, having sired some
children, even if he doesn't play much of a paternal role in their lives.
In short, the arrangement of these eight letters—the same eight letters
for both words—can take a man in different directions.§§

A good parent, for example, is supposed to be responsible, nurtur-
ing, and protective of his children. That's our intuitive sense of the
assignment, or perhaps the one we guilt ourselves into accepting, and
most people would list these among the job's basic requirements. Our
problem is not that a good pater (or a good father, since *pater* is such a
weird word) isn't supposed to meet these same requirements; it's that a
father might be asked to do—or be—something *else* as well. Something
more. A father might have equally compelling paternal requirements to
honor, in other words: alternative objectives that could even tend to
clash with his parental sensibilities.

Men feel this conflict because, as research indicates, fathers express
a distinctive and different style of caregiving. In particular, fathers are
more inclined to play with their kids in unconventional ways, relying

---

§§ While we're at it, it's worth noting (in a note, no less) that *prenatal* also shares these
same letters. Which seems unfair in a way, because if anyone deserves verbal
association with *that* word, shouldn't it be women/mothers?

less on traditional modes or methods and gravitating more toward what scholars refer to as "activation-exploration themes." In this spirit, dads are more likely to push boundaries as a means of promoting positive, prosocial attitudes and behaviors, especially in young boys and even while roughhousing—which, as studies indicate, has the potential to establish brain-cell connections and, therefore, build intelligence.

This distinction frames our concerns for this chapter, because a father hopes to meet the expectations of both roles while conceding the challenges of joint membership. A dad feels torn between the competing impulses of the *parental* way, focusing on caution, emphasizing restraint, thinking about consequences, and generally proceeding in a manner described in manuals on the subject, and the *paternal* way, opting for excitement, relishing spontaneity, thinking (differently) about consequences, and looking for fun in a manner no sane publisher would ever include in a manual on the subject.

Ideally, a father finds a way to reconcile his impulses; but sometimes he's pulled too far in one direction. And that one direction is usually the paternal direction—making him, by some accounts, a good father but a bad parent. It's complicated.

A Battle of Wills

I WILL ADMIT IT WAS a poor choice of breakfast fare, but I had to get ready for work. With Wills being inordinately needy this particular morning, I decided to buy a few extra minutes of peace by placating him with something he would *want* to eat. This nutritious spectacle, never once featured in a parenting magazine, involved a piece of bread topped with nearly a jar of grape jelly, also known as purple sugar.

It seemed like a good idea at the time. With a desirable morning dining option, I reasoned, he might be more inclined to stay seated while I did some minimal grooming upstairs. I took out extra insurance on this prospect by turning on his favorite cartoon, *The Berenstain Bears*. This wasn't a bad idea in theory; but in practice, Wills was so mesmerized by

Brother Bear's antics that he missed his mouth with almost every handful of jelly, while forgoing the bread altogether. At a clip of about three handfuls every ten seconds, it wasn't long before his face resembled the battle-ready mug of Mel Gibson's character in *Braveheart*.

Hearing him declare himself "all done" and realizing he would soon be walking around the house looking for things to touch, stopping by Lucas's room to shatter various LEGO creations, and depositing some of my important papers in the trashcan, I rushed downstairs to contain the damage. I didn't see the boy in his usual hiding places, but I did notice a grape-colored path of slime running along the walls going into the kitchen.

Using my expert powers of inference to conclude that's where he was, I found him wedged between the wall and the *open* door of the refrigerator. He didn't seem to understand that the door of an appliance containing cold air looks unusual, and thus suspicious, when it's left open. Nor did he seem to understand that it looks funny when two little feet are poking out from underneath that open door.

As I approached, he became still. (I didn't know he could do that.)

As I called out, he became silent. (I didn't know he could do that, either.)

I then made a dramatic speech, promising to put in a good word for him if he would surrender without incident. This caused him to look around the refrigerator door and lock eyes with me—just as the theme music to *The Good, the Bad and the Ugly* began playing quietly in the background.

I have you, I thought.

You don't have me, he thought.

I heard you think that, I thought.

I'm invisible, he thought.

The boy's confidence was awe-inspiring but totally misplaced. How could he think I didn't have him? He had no escape—and nor was he invisible.

What was his plan? Did he think he could make it to the state line? Then what? I'm Dad. I'm in charge everywhere.

You have no chance, I thought.

You don't have me, he thought. Again.

I heard you think that, I thought. Again.

I can teleport, he thought.

Clearly, the sensible thing would be to just give up. I would prosecute, for sure, but only posture minimally during the press conference. I would even recommend leniency at sentencing. He could do his "time"-out, find God, and plead for mercy before the Parole Board when she came home from work that evening. The Parole Board was known for her mercy, especially when guilty parties cuddled with her and professed actual innocence.

But I knew he would never surrender. I knew that because *I* would never surrender—and I pretty much made him this way. Emily's better nature is in there, somewhere, but this kid is a pain in the butt because I'm a pain in the butt. The upside of our frequent showdowns is that I have learned his ways. Or maybe I just know his ways because they're my own ways. Either way, I know what he's thinking.

He's planning to sprint by me, burst into the living room, and then dive headfirst onto the couch. For some reason, he thinks he's "safe" there, as if it were home base in a game of Tag. By this square logic that he was trying to force into a round hole, if he could just reach a point twenty-five feet away from here, I wouldn't be able to get him anymore.

But there was no way I was going to let that happen. With his face still covered in jelly, he presented a genuine threat to the home. If he reached the couch, he would treat that poor piece of furniture like an escape tunnel, burrowing into the cushions for protection. And considering the existing collection of popcorn kernels, raisins, and cheese stick crumbles in those crevices, any added insult of purple goo would surely void the warranty from IKEA. Which the Scandinavian stick figure on the bottom of the couch made abundantly clear with some horribly distressed images and a host of violent exclamation marks.

This is precisely the sort of parental/paternal conflict referenced above. I knew that I needed to clean up the jelly and end all this non-sense, as a good parent would; but I also felt I needed to save face, as a good father (or pater) should.

The parental voice in me was saying, with predictable apprehension, *Control the situation and set a good example.*

But the paternal voice came back with something else, insisting, *Screw that. Just make an example of him!*

How could I say no to that? A father wants his son to grow up to be a good person, one who understands manners, morals, and general rules of conduct, but he also wants his boy to grow up to be a man. And sometimes men do the wrong things for the right reasons. Some-times they act as less in order to be more. Sometimes they take the low road in order to keep little people from getting all high and mighty. Again, it's complicated.

But for some guidance on this matter, a way to evaluate the options, consider the present situation in the context of the rest of his life. What would Wills take away from this episode? What lesson would he learn from his own provocation and from my response to it?

Do we "set a good example" on the battlefield, or do we fight like hell and try to survive? In combat, are we out of danger just because we dive onto a couch? Hardly. The enemy keeps shooting at us, even if we're hiding under a cushion, and we do the same. Until one or both of us die(s). Fight and live to fight another day. *That* is the lesson.

So, you see, I could have just walked away. But I also couldn't. Not if I was to be a good dad by proving to this little preschooler that, in fact, he's not the indomitable force he's presumed himself to be since birth. If I didn't take care of him here, in the right way and with gusto, then next time he might try to hide *inside* the refrigerator. Because he might pretend it was a teleport machine.

After giving the matter a few seconds of consideration, I realized the correct response in this situation. It might not be pretty, but it had to be done. I called Wills out and moved into battle mode.

BEFORE WE GO ON, take a moment to recall some of the signature films of the 1980s. During this decade, when our only concerns were famine, nuclear war, AIDS, and acid rain, Hollywood provided us with cinematic gems such as *Over the Top*, where Sylvester Stallone drove a truck and arm wrestled for cash; *Mannequin*, where Andrew McCarthy fell in love with a plastic person; *Ishtar*, where Warren Beatty and Dustin Hoffman wandered the desert for some reason; and *Red Dawn*, where high school kids battled Soviet paratroopers who were invading the state of Colorado.

As entertaining as those movies were, however, *The Karate Kid* stood above them all—and on only one leg, no less. Because of this classic feature, adolescent males began unhealthy obsessions with Elisabeth Shue, and enrollments in martial-arts classes skyrocketed. No one cared about the supposed differences between karate, judo, taekwondo, and so on; they just wanted to kick some shit and look like ninjas. All that mumbo jumbo from Mr. Miyagi was definitely a drag, but the closing scenes of the movie made all the manual labor worth it. In those final minutes were several important truths about life: good guys, bad guys, strengths, weaknesses, and Elisabeth Shue looking fantastic.

And in the simulation of those scenes about to take place in our kitchen, so too were there several of life's important truths about to be revealed. Which I knew Wills would realize, because we'd watched this movie together. He didn't follow much of the plot, but of course he was mesmerized by the final match, understanding exactly how the end of the film dictated what was about to occur between us.

I didn't have a black band tied around my head, but for the role-playing exercise I was about to initiate with my younger son, I took on the combined parts of both the sensei and Johnny (the blond guy), while Wills was Ralph Macchio's Daniel. In that spirit, and as we stood there facing each other, I issued to myself the film's (in)famous fight-scene command, "Sweep the leg," followed up that command by giving myself a look of alarm at the prospect of leveling a preschooler in such a completely chicken-shit way, and then reluctantly accepted my duty, readied my stance, and swept his leg.

Well, you know what I mean. I didn't *really* sweep his leg. Come on, we're just talking about promoting prosocial behaviors and establishing brain-cell connections, remember? Not child abuse. All I did was grab his shoulder, slide my foot behind his leg, and gently lower him to the ground until he was nothing more than a pile of pajamas and jelly.

Then I left the kitchen so he could spend some time thinking about how he got into this mess by making a mess. I hoped he might use this opportunity to reflect on his life, especially the ways he could make better choices. (Isn't that what a good parent would do?)

Within seconds, however, he was already calling me back into the kitchen. He said he wanted to "tell" me something, which was his usual way of saying he wanted to ask me something, show me a magic trick, or do a somersault. But not this time.

Indeed, when I got back in there, I found him standing upright with both arms over his head. He had his leg up, effecting a crane pose (sort of), and the ferocious look on his face said: *Come at me, old man.*

That made me smile, because, seriously, could there be anything more adorable than a little boy with the chutzpah to attempt a crane pose? Yes, this all started because he wouldn't eat a real breakfast, slathered himself in purple goo, escaped confinement, hid from the authorities, dismissed the opportunity for detente, fought the law, lost to the law, and had his leg swept—and yet, here he was baiting me with a foot cocked and ready.

My parental voice was pleading: *Just be done with this. You're already late for work. Besides, you can't teach him to solve problems by copying fight scenes from movies. Grow up, dude!*

But my paternal voice was broadcasting much louder, demanding: *Are you kidding me? Don't you remember that Kenny Rogers song about the boy who took crap his whole life until he finally let the Gatlin boys have it? Quit being such a pussy and sweep the other leg!*

Counting that as yet another win for the paternal side, I came at him and . . . well, you've seen the movie, right?

Boys Will Be Boys

I'M SURE YOU AREN'T supposed to throw snowballs at your kids while hiding in a spot behind the shed, a spot they've never even seen. I'm sure you aren't supposed to pretend to be occupied with some mundane garden task as they sneak up on you with water guns, only to find themselves devastated with a front-side blast from the hose. And I'm also sure you aren't supposed to take pride in using your considerably greater weight to knock them over on the trampoline, even though they love it and ask for it all the time.

"They could get hurt!" Emily always says, which they do, in fact—but which they also do while playing soccer, skateboarding, climbing trees, trying to catch the football, and pretty much any other activity they're involved with throughout the day. Wills has even been known to get hurt just sitting in a chair. Not falling out of a chair—just sitting in one. He even held the unofficial record for "incident reports" (forms documenting injuries) at his preschool, averaging over three per week during his most statistically impossible period.

What can explain this? What accounts for this recklessness, rambunctiousness, and restlessness? Are these qualities wired in? Is it the influence of the Y chromosome? Is it just that boys will be boys?

Perhaps this notion seems passé to you, but that doesn't mean it isn't true—or that there isn't at least some truth to it. Certainly, plenty of girls are also reckless, rambunctious, and restless, while plenty of boys are not; but there is a wealth of academic literature indicating that—by nature, nurture, or both—boys behave differently, especially in their penchant for rough-and-tumble physical play. In fact, as the author of the epigraph to this chapter observes in her book on the male brain, boys interact in a significantly more physical fashion, wrestling, play-fighting, and looking for ways to overpower one another up to six times as much as girls do.

Boys like to fly down the slide as fast as they can, ride the swing as high as it goes, and be flown around like Superman. Pretty much all the time, it seems. Which are memories they recall fondly once they grow up and begin returning the favor for the next generation of boys being boys. At least until they slip a disc in their back. Or drop a kid on the way down. Or send one of them through a wall.

Um, yeah. A wall.

ALLOW ME TO EXPLAIN. The game was called Eye-*YAH*—as in the exhalation one makes during martial-arts exhibitions. I'm not exactly sure how to spell this made-up game, but that was how it was pronounced. The gist of this nightly ritual was that a little, medium, and big boy would wrestle on the big boy's king-size bed: pillow fighting, jumping, flipping, falling, pile driving, and plenty of other things that are a terrible idea right before bedtime.

The rules were often in flux, but biting was always unacceptable, as were kicks to the "nuts" (their word, not mine). Punching was never allowed, but light pounding was okay. Otherwise, there were pillows to the face, wedgies, ice cubes in the shorts, plenty of tickling, blood-curdling battle cries, flops by the big boy (to boost the confidence of the little and medium ones), and general mayhem.

Which is where the wall comes in. The details of this particular episode are murky, because I've kept them that way, but basically a little boy was sent flying through the air over a bed, after which he landed on an exercise ball and bounced toward the wall—hitting it while upside-down and puncturing the surface as if it were paper.

Oh, and the little boy was also wearing high heels.

Yes, I'm serious. Who could make *that* up?

It's important to stress that the game was really confusing that night. Bodies were flying around, there was a lot of noise, and the bed was a disaster zone with pillows, a comforter, and sheets all over the place. Plus, the exercise ball usually stored in the closet had somehow been thrown into the mix, serving as both a cannonball to be shot from ground level and a bomb to be dropped from the ceiling.

Because he liked the idea of firing the ball, Lucas, the medium boy, was holding the implement on one side of the bed, crouching close to the floor and waiting for the right opportunity to launch it. Meanwhile, Wills, the little boy, had for some reason gone into the closet and come out, so to speak, wearing a pair of Emily's high heels.

I can't say that I was entirely happy with this turn of events, where my preschool son was shaking his hips back and forth along an imagined catwalk in the bedroom, but my love for him is unconditional. If high heels are in his future, so be it.

What was most amazing is that, even *in* those high heels, this boy still had swagger. How a lad could manage that while wearing ladies' footwear, I don't know. Somehow though, he had it going—and he kept letting me know that I had it coming. Baiting me, as always.

My parental impulse was pushing me to take things down a notch. A good parent should realize that, with all these incendiary elements, a great conflagration could ensue. *Would* ensue, actually.

At the same time, my paternal impulse was reminding me of all the moves I used to watch Hulk Hogan do when I was a kid and proposing the specific maneuvers most appropriate for dealing with a shit-talking youngster now wobbling around in high heels.

In a previous battle, I might have—ahem—*let* the little boy win. Perhaps because that crane pose had been so cute. But not this time. And so, as Wills came at me, I scooped him up, gave him a wedgie with my left hand, hoisted him above my head, and prepared to send him flying onto the bed and into a pile of pillows.

The problem was, Lucas was still crouching by the bed, armed with the exercise ball and ready to fire at *anything* coming into the airspace over the mattress. Which meant that when I launched Wills, Lucas launched the ball—or rolled the ball, actually, and not with much force, leading it to stop right where Wills was about to land.

We pause to ensure the pieces are properly arranged in your mind. There was a little boy wearing high heels. While roughhousing in a way that helped him develop prosocial behaviors and establish brain-cell connections, this little boy was corralled by an extremely loving, often responsible big boy and tossed a few feet above a very soft mattress on a cushiony bed with LOTS of pillows.

And yet, without intending any harm, an otherwise cautious medium boy propelled a big exercise ball just hard enough for it to stop right where the airborne little boy was about to come down—leading the small human projectile to land on what was effectively a spherical trampoline and then bounce off the device while flying through space with enough force to careen forward, flip upside-down, and ultimately hit the wall *feet*-first, before bracing his landing with outstretched hands as he collapsed into all those pillows.

It looked somewhat like this:

Do you know what happens when drywall meets a thirty-five-pound missile wearing high heels?

Drywall loses.

Well, to be more exact, drywall blows up. It does not get simply scratched, poked, or pierced; it gets obliterated. It gives up a hole eight inches wide for the involved parties to stare at in a mixture of awe and terror. And perhaps most fascinating of all, it does this while holding on to a piece of footwear—leaving a dress shoe sticking out of the wall as if it were the handle to a trap door.

Upon impact, it was quiet for a few lifelong moments. The crowd watched to see if Evel Knievel was all right, and the medium and big boys wet their pants. Wills was surely accustomed to flying around and pushing the limits, but the way this went down—which is to say, the way he went up and then went down—was extreme even by his standards. Never before had he actually gone through a wall.

Lucas started crying, because Mommy already hated this game and now Daddy was *really* in trouble. And Daddy started looking for sheets to tie together so he could escape out the window, seeing this as most likely the end of a nonincarcerated life. But Wills didn't get the memo about being terrified.

The small human who had forged a new way into the attic with his feet was wriggling around in the pile of pillows and—you guessed it— laughing hysterically. With absolutely no appreciation for what had just happened, no conception of luck, no understanding of physics, no awareness of the fact that little boys aren't supposed to be doing home demolition in high heels, all he could do was utter, with breathless enthusiasm: "Wow! That was awesome! Can we do it again?"

This made me think. (Not always a good thing.)

My paternal voice immediately suggested: *Hmmmmm, good question, Wills. Maybe this time with a blindfold?*

Fortunately, however, my parental voice quickly shut down the entire discussion. Emily had just gotten home, and it was time to start coming up with a story. She wasn't going to care about brain-cell connections with an enormous hole in the wall. And she wouldn't be moved by talk of prosocial behaviors with gypsum dust and pieces of insulation all over our bed. She was just going to be really pissed off— which she was, sending me to sleep on the couch that night. Right next to the jelly.

ACCOMPANIED MINORS

We have a very full flight today, and it looks like I won't be able to seat you all together. I can put Dad in the front and Mom and the boys in the back of the plane.

-a helpful ticket agent

THEY ALWAYS CONCLUDE the announcements by inviting us to "sit back, relax, and enjoy the flight." But why? And how? Shouldn't captain and crew know better than to tease the possibility of a pleasant experience in the air? They fly all day long, several days per week. They see the glares, witness the air rage, feel the tension, and register both the passive- and aggressive-aggression on every flight.

Is this just wishful thinking? It's not that a pleasant flight wouldn't be nice; it's just that it's increasingly hard to imagine. Those of us in the coach section would love to "sit back," if only the guy behind us wasn't using one of those devices that stops us from reclining the seat. We might try to "relax," once we have surveyed the other passengers and located those most likely to have a psychotic episode. And we would be delighted to "enjoy" the flight, if only we weren't being charged for everything except the air we need to breathe (as of this writing).

So, what can such a statement actually mean if it's nearly impossible for it to mean what they pretend it means? Why all the wasted words falling on deaf ears? Do the airlines keep up this charade because the expression is written into the script for takeoff? Is it something so habitual that members of the crew don't even realize they're saying it— such a part of the routine and pre-flight ritual that it comes out reflexively, like "Gesundheit" follows a sneeze? Have they simply stopped listening to themselves, like the rest of us have, especially when they're demonstrating the safety features of the airplane?

Or could it be that their perspective is skewed by the fact that, when they encourage us to do these things, they happen to be standing amidst comfortable passengers in the first-class cabin? Do they assume that if *those* passengers look happy, with their ample leg room, private lavatory, free drinks, and protective fabric barrier, then we must all be experiencing the same moment of Zen? If so, I would suggest they pull back the curtain and have a look at how things have changed.

IN THE GOOD OLD DAYS, flying was cost-prohibitive for most individuals, their bodies were smaller, safety protocols and regulations either didn't exist or were underenforced, and an enjoyable flight probably *was* the norm. Air travel was a glamorous affair: the province of the few and the proud, the well-to-do, and the perpetually put-together. Perky stewardesses—not flight attendants, *stewardesses*—gratuitously enabled vices with offers like "Another drink, sir?" and "Could I get you a clean ashtray?"; the captain handed out little wings that would actually stick to something; travelers carried suitcases emblazoned with stamps from exotic locations; lobster was served for breakfast, lunch, and dinner; and federal law prohibited children from crying, kicking seats, or spilling juice.

But now air travel is the province of the many and the lowly, the weak and the weary, and the large and in charge. Tank tops are the attire of choice; suitcases can't be emblazoned with stamps from exotic locations, because they've been mashed beyond recognition in overhead compartments; your "lobster" is actually Patagonian Toothfish available in a snack box for thirty-nine dollars; flight attendants—not stewardesses, *flight attendants*—are no longer objects of fantasy; and children cry, whine, and torment fellow passengers almost as much as their adult counterparts do.

Faced with this as our new normal, why are we so slow to adjust? Why have we shown such collective cognitive dissonance about air travel? Why haven't we adopted any of the more realistic expectations that we maintain about other modes of transit?

Like moving around the country by bus, for example. Buses provide budget-conscious thrill-seekers with a fabulous option for their travels. They are an essential part of our interstate-transportation system—and, at least in the lower forty-eight states, buses can deliver you to the same places the airlines can. But still, seriously, think about it: When you go Greyhound, does the driver ever invite you to "sit back, relax, and enjoy the ride"?

No, of course not.

Is that because Greyhound doesn't have an attendant handing out little bags with only three pretzels? Or is it because bus companies know their role and are therefore realistic enough not to overpromise and underdeliver? Greyhound doesn't prohibit you from enjoying your trip from Little Rock to Kansas City for seventeen dollars but nor does it presume that's likely to happen.

Given that the airlines have effectively become the bus companies of the sky, perhaps it's time for carriers to update their text and present a more plausible pre-flight announcement—one that rests on fact not fiction. Something more like this: "We know this whole experience sucks, but we still get you there faster than anyone else. Just take a pill, don't pass any gas, and don't press that damn button for any reason. This will all be over in a few hours."

That message would tell us what to really expect out of the trip. And it would also concede the reality that, with any sort of progress, there is a certain amount of regress: acknowledging that, while air travel may be so "easy" these days, it's also an immense pain in the ass. A pain in the ass perhaps not even worth the effort, to be honest, especially since people now tend to fly just because they *can*. Because the option exists.

Back in the nineteenth century, by contrast, parents rolled their kids across the continent in covered wagons, enduring attacks by tribes, scarlet fever, brutally cold winters, intensely hot summers, limited rations, dangerous drinking water, cougars, and campfire sing-alongs. The journey wasn't pleasant but nor did people travel as they do today.

Rather, they went on one long trip, realized how awful it was, settled down, and probably never took another discretionary venture again. The covered wagon kept things in check: it wasn't convenient moving around from here to there, so people didn't do it very much.

But now it's all so wonderfully simple and inviting, isn't it? The deals on the travel websites are so enticing, the miles earned with credit card usage so alluring. When you're thinking about your next trip—and, conveniently, not thinking about your previous trips—it seems so easy that you decide to go for it. If you had regular reminders to the contrary, like arrows buzzing by your head or viruses tearing you apart, as families did while riding along in covered wagons, you might never get on another plane. But when the airlines tempt you by letting you board first if you are traveling with young children, how can you resist?

What's more, as a parent in the twenty-first century, you don't need to load provisions for a five-month journey that will be terrible and that you might not even survive.

You just need to pack every imaginable toy, book, instrument, or device that could distract a child for a minute or two during a several-hours-long passage through the air.

And then you need to avoid causing a scene when half the stuff you packed to distract the child doesn't make it through Security, taking care not to launch into tirades when the playdough is taken from the bag because it could secretly be a package of C-4 explosives.

And then you need to be ready to put a positive spin on the loss of favorite toys that were left in the seat pocket of an airplane now on its way to Abu Dhabi.

And then you need to ride the escalator for five hours on a layover.

And then you need to be the parent who wins the game of Rock, Paper, Scissors so that you won't have to deal with the diaper-form devastation threatening to clear out the entire left side of the plane.

And then you need to act as a deputy enforcing rules that even you barely understand, asserting, "I don't know, dude. You just have to turn it off for the first ten minutes even though the other things can be left on for some reason."

And then you need to become a party to discrimination, insisting, "No, you *can't* use the bathroom we walked by on the way to our seat. People like us have to use a separate bathroom."

And then you need to invent a justification for this awful injustice, explaining, "I know that doesn't sound like the world Martin Luther King, Jr. had in mind, but the airplane lives in a different world."

And then you need to top it all off with an utterly hopeless request, pleading, "For Pete's sake, stop burping the alphabet! People are trying to sit back, relax, and enjoy the flight, okay?"

For Your Security

YOU CAN THINK ABOUT how it's all so easy these days the next time you're at the airport. There will be plenty of time while you wait in line and plenty of lines to give you enough time. The airport is all about lines. To go somewhere by air, you must first spend considerable time going nowhere.

The upside of all this standing around is that you can take a moment, or many moments, to coach the kids on what they're about to see—much of which is confusing and some of which is alarming. In this regard, it could be that some parents sit a toddler down and give him the straight talk about how bad guys like to hurt people by blowing up or shooting at the very type of plane the family is about to board.

But most probably don't. Most parents likely just present rules without reasoning and then require compliance from little people who are not old enough to have known things any other way. To have seen the way it used to be. To recall a time without so many restrictions.

Some children will be fine with this direction, accepting instructions in the same way they follow—but do not endorse—rules in the school lunchroom that prohibit them from buying fifteen chocolate milks.

But others will not.

Others will ask questions.

Or fail to listen.

Or listen but not hear.

Or hear but ignore.

Or follow the rules but not really in the way you would like—perhaps lacking the discernment necessary to avoid taking directives to an illogical end.

One solution here, a way to reconcile a child's limited capability with a parent's ultimate culpability, is to adopt a system that charts the way to a desired result through a series of deliberate actions. As in the way medical professionals, for example, conduct themselves in advance of an operation. This form of preparation calls for involved parties to proceed through a checklist whereby a proposition is offered and an audible assent is required to move on to each next step.

"We're here to work on the patient named John Doe," whoever is in charge might say as the procedure is about to begin. "And we're operating on his *right* leg not his left leg," this boss would add, among several other items, before finishing with the signature element at each step during any such checklist: "Do we all agree?"

As research indicates, this idea—and especially the ritualized nature of its implementation—has the potential to cut down on mistakes, missed steps, and other errors attributable to deviations from protocol. Self-reminders and structured preconditions of official acknowledgement keep warnings and objectives top of mind.

Because flying with children presents its own chaos and unforeseen circumstances, rivaling an operation in its range of emotions, while also involving endless hurrying, waiting, swearing, and random people in uniforms, the checklist method can be quite helpful. Getting kids onto the plane to begin the fun family vacation isn't the same as determining which leg to amputate, but this is a difference of degree not kind.

Consider adopting the checklist below the next time you fly somewhere with your kids. It can't make things any worse, right? Right?

Airport Security Screening Checklist

✓ We would like to board the plane. Do we all agree?

✓ We will do what the people with blue shirts tell us to do even if other people with blue shirts tell us to do something different. Do we all agree?

✓ We are going to stand still, be patient in line, and not play with the Tensabarrier that herds us around like cattle. Do we all agree?

✓ We are going to wait in our first line until the person holding the marker and flashlight waves us forward. Do we all agree?

✓ No matter how awkward the interaction is with the marker-and-flashlight person, we will respond appropriately. Do we all agree?

✓ Once we get past the person with the marker and flashlight, we are not going to climb into a gray bin and try to ride through the thing-washing machine. Do we all agree?

✓ But we *are* going to put all of our things—even things we'd prefer to hold, like stuffies—inside those gray bins and wave *bye-bye* to them as they go through the washer. Do we all agree?

✓ Once our things are all clean, we are going to stand still and wait for the signal from another person with a blue shirt who will tell us it's safe to walk through the mystery door. Do we all agree?

✓ After we get through the mystery door, we're going to stand still and not touch anything, not lick anything, not poke anyone, not roll around on the floor, not ask the people with blue shirts things like "Where are all the bad guys?" and not try to walk *back* through the mystery door to do it again. Do we all agree?

✓ Also, if (when) Dad is pulled aside for additional screening, we are not going to laugh while the strange little man waves the wand around and touches him in places usually reserved only for Mom. Do we all agree?

✓ Finally, we are not going to make any jokes. Even if we hear other people making a joke—or trying to make a joke. Especially people with blue shirts. Jokes are "not appreciated" at Security. Besides, there's nothing funny about flying with kids. Do we all agree?

WITH AGREEMENT ON THE TERMS, it's now time for action. A family in this position has talked through the various phases still to come and has anticipated likely complications. Once they reach the front of the line jointly utilized by child-breeders and the disabled, the members of this traveling party can begin the screening process.

The first and most challenging step here involves satisfying the gatekeeper. This is the man—it's almost always a man—who sits on a stool, holds a flashlight and marker, and makes squiggles on boarding passes. The gatekeeper wears a blue shirt like the rest of the wonderful people who keep us safe, and he takes his job very seriously.

He is trained to ferret out danger, which he does by establishing a degree of initial, if still short-lived, rapport with traveling parties. And his effort to build such a relationship with people who would prefer not to have a relationship with him at all usually proceeds along one of two primary tracks: he either asks a straightforward question—perhaps inquiring about the weather or the origins of a passenger's curious-sounding last name—or he tries to make a joke.

"NEVADA?!" the gatekeeper might exclaim when handed a driver's license from the state of sin. "Man, I remember this one crazy night in Reno," he might add, before reaching denouement with a devious smile, a wink, and a coy confession like, "Oh, wait—actually, I *don't*."

This, of course, would be his humorous way of letting you know that federal workers really know how to party; but it would also be where we might depend on the behavior anticipated by that checklist. A question about the day's precipitation is one thing, and speculation about your family ancestry might be another. You could just answer those honestly or make up a convincing story.

A *joke*, however, is an action from the gatekeeper that requires a specific type of reaction from you. You can't just say, "Well, since I'm wet, it must be raining out there" or "My great-grandfather came from the North Pole, so I guess I'm North Polish." You have to give the gatekeeper a *laugh*. Or at least a chuckle. Okay, maybe just a smile.

As an adult knows, when the gatekeeper tries to be funny, it means he thinks he has some good material. Even when the adult thinks the joke is dumb, or that the gatekeeper would only be funny if compared to a comedian like Carrot Top, a grown-up possesses the discretion to offer at least the *appearance* of amusement. If nothing else, an adult realizes that if he doesn't play along, he will seem suspicious—which means the gatekeeper will start flicking the corner of his driver's license like East German border guards used to do in spy movies.

But do children know this? Kids would have agreed to respond "appropriately" while going through the checklist process only minutes before, but that's a long time ago in the mind of a child. Would kids recognize *this* as the sort of moment when their most appropriate demonstration of *appropriate* might be necessary?

Would they realize they were supposed to laugh (not cry) when the gatekeeper greeted them with his best impression of Elmer Fudd? Would they know the weird comment delivered with the weird voice from the weird man was supposed to be amusing, not alarming?

In the same spirit, would they know when *not* to laugh—when, as the signs say, jokes are "not appreciated," despite the fact that the gatekeeper keeps telling them? That is, would they understand that when the gatekeeper asks, "Hey there, partner, you don't have a machine gun in that little backpack of yours, do you?" they are not supposed to begin howling like a preschool lunatic?

Probably not. How could kids know what to expect when adults don't? Sometimes the gatekeeper is Groucho Marx, going for the funny bone, and sometimes he's Joe Friday, wanting only the facts. You never can tell until you reach the front of the line and he begins his horribly odd and utterly unpredictable ritual of interacting with little people.

As the gatekeeper sees it, while children aren't quite like adults in their actual potential to inflict catastrophic harm, they could still be accomplices in a larger conspiracy. Half pints are still full-value prospects, in other words; and a child—who generally lacks the photo identification that would make this entire ordeal unnecessary—won't get through the gate until he gives its keeper some kind of proof that he really *is* who his boarding pass says he is. Which is to say, that he actually does, in fact, belong to the adult standing next to him.

Styles for ascertaining this ostensible connection vary, but the most common manner is for the gatekeeper to simply look at a little boy standing before him, point to the large man standing next to him, and ask, "Young man, is this your daddy?"—an inquiry delivered with a glance at the large man that warns: *Do not attempt to influence the witness.*

This probably seems like an easy enough question, but it isn't.

Or at least it isn't for a certain little boy I know.

It's true that your average preschooler, looking up at your average dad, looking back at the strange man with the flashlight and the marker who is, for some reason, asking him to identify his father, *should* be able to handle this.

But what if you don't have an average preschooler?

What if, instead, you have the most *non*-average preschooler in the world? What if you have the type of child who fixes things that are upside-down by turning them inside-out—the sort of boy who would still be the class clown even at clown school? And what if this non-average preschooler got an "easy enough" question along these lines, smiled (of course), and then said, "N*ooooooooooooooooooooooooooooooooo*"?

Would that be an "appropriate" response?

No, of course not.

Would that matter to the non-average preschooler?

No, of course not.

Would it matter to the gatekeeper?

Yeah, it would.

A more forgiving gatekeeper might let this one pass, realizing he's probably got enough to document paternity based on the fact that, only minutes before, the little boy was up on the large man's shoulders— and also because the little boy looks a hell of a lot like the large man.

But not every keeper of the gate would feel that way. A less forgiving gatekeeper might not be sold on the relationship at all, justifying his need for additional proof on the basis that terror can come in many sizes and safety must come first. Even before sanity.

The long line of individuals waiting to go through this gate might feel otherwise, each of them lamenting the fantastic simplicity of air travel these days, but a gatekeeper needing more assurance before bestowing that squiggle on the little boy's boarding pass might decide to regroup and take another shot at it.

"Well then, young man, *who* is your daddy?" the gatekeeper might ask as a follow-up question, not realizing he's made things worse.

Reframing the question in this way probably makes sense within the confines of gatekeeper logic, but that's because their training doesn't cover non-average preschoolers. If the little person before him deliberately missed on "*Is* this your daddy?" what on earth would he do with a question that let him fill in the blank with any name in the world?

A game of Who's your daddy? with a non-average preschooler could begin with reasonable responses like God or Geronimo, but soon the child would be suggesting names like Mr. Magoo, Harry Potter, and Mrs. Butterworth.

Which would be a problem for *everyone*, actually, because the family cannot get going on the fun family vacation until the gatekeeper lets them pass; and all the rest of the travelers—all the normal people—came to the airport on this particular morning for the purpose of going somewhere else. The airport is not a destination unto itself.

As such, the best hope for all parties involved would be for the non-average preschooler to simply forget he was playing a game at all: for him to suddenly feel hungry, have to go to the bathroom, or get impatient with this situation of his own doing—and for him to then turn to the large man next to him, demanding to know, even louder than usual: "Daaaaaaaaaaaaaaaaaaaaaaaaaaaaaaaad, why aren't we *going* anywhere?!"

Bingo. Squiggle granted.

This isn't quite the way the vetting process is described in the manual for gatekeepers; but on this day, it would be enough to pass. Or at least not to fail. It would be enough to let the family members move on to the mystery door, where they could empty their pockets, take off their clothes, bear a quick molestation, be pulled aside for who the hell knows why, get dressed again, wait in another line to board the plane, note the pained looks of fellow passengers disdainful of children, locate their seats, and get ready for even more fun as the flight attendant—not the stewardess, the *flight attendant*—concluded the announcements by inviting them to "sit back, relax, and enjoy the flight."

VOICES IN MY HEAD

First you will come to the Sirens who enchant all who come near them. If anyone unwarily draws in too close and hears the singing of the Sirens, his wife and children will never welcome him home again, for they sit in a green field and warble him to death with the sweetness of their song. There is a great heap of dead men's bones lying all around, with the flesh still rotting off them. Therefore, pass these Sirens by, and stop your men's ears with wax that none of them may hear; but if you like you can listen yourself, for you may get the men to bind you as you stand upright on a cross-piece half way up the mast, and they must lash the rope's ends to the mast itself, that you may have the pleasure of listening. If you beg and pray the men to unloose you, then they must bind you faster.

-Homer

WHEN LUCAS WAS SEVEN, meaning he was not so old the songs were uncool, and Wills was four, meaning he had a basic grasp of their meaning, we would constantly have children's music CDs playing in the car. Sometimes, I would try to drown out the lyrics by revving the engine, but often I had no choice but to listen: no opportunity to resist as the songs seeped in, got me thinking, and were stored away forever as voices in my head.

Music has incredible power. Songs can inspire, entertain, and bring joy. But they can also be their own form of torture, which is why the American military used rock 'n' roll music against former dictator Manuel Noriega while he was hiding out in the Holy See's embassy in Panama. And it's also why the military's Psychological Operations Company used ballads from *Barney & Friends* to deprive POWs of sleep during the second war in Iraq—giving us proof once and for all that, while everyone's favorite purple dinosaur might occasionally make a child smile, he can also shatter the soul of an adult.

If children's music is powerful enough to make prisoners of war divulge information they don't even have just to make it stop, how does an ordinary father stand a chance? He may not be "warbled" to death by the sweetness of song, as Homer's Sirens disposed of their victims; but unless he's "stopped" his ears with wax, he can't resist.

The songs just keep pushing. And pushing. And pushing. Until they eventually break through. And when that happens, when a father takes that tragic turn, it's only a matter of time before he becomes preoccupied trying to make sense of the lyrics in these offerings, repeatedly wondering: *Wait a minute—how could a tortoise and a ladybug float down the stream on a leaf? The physics is impossible. The tortoise is too heavy to ride the leaf at all, and the ladybug is too small to offer a reasonable counterbalance.*

You see?

It can get that bad.

This man could have been thinking about important things, like why NHL franchises are popular in cities with warmer climates, but now he's got these stupid voices in his head. And he can't get them out. At this point, it's only a matter of time before he goes over the edge with something worthy of institutional commitment, perhaps considering: *For that matter, why in the world are a tortoise and a ladybug hanging out in the first place? Tortoises aren't friends with bugs. Actually, don't they eat bugs?*

It's true that these songs are for kids and should be granted some liberties here and there, but like a pledge or any other spoken ritual, lyrics get reinforced through repetition. The danger is that an audience might take what it hears as audio gospel. Which means a song might be considered presumptively legitimate until proven otherwise—and sometimes even after proven otherwise.

Just to be clear, we aren't talking about songs dealing with *fantasy* subjects like aliens, fairies, and elves. Those creatures are not of this world and, as such, enjoy their own fantastic terms of engagement— their own reality and their own rules. In Elflandia, the population can somersault through the air on unicorns and we can't say a damn thing about it, because that's just what elves and unicorns do when they're feeling happy.

We are only referring to songs of this world, songs speaking to our own reality. It's not that ditties for kids must be totally believable, of course (What child honestly likes to "eat, eat, eat apples and bananas"?); it's just that they shouldn't be totally unbelievable. It's one thing for *elves* to fly, in other words, but a song about a flying bear wouldn't make sense, would it? Bears don't fly. They just warn people against starting forest fires and then maul them to death.

To ensure impressionable children hear things right, it's important for adults to intercede and interrogate the musical messages vying for space in a youngster's brain. As unhinged as it may seem to subject familiar standards and comfortable classics to the test for truth, it's better than little ones growing up and believing some of the nonsense coming out of their mouths as they innocently sing along. This is about saving kids from themselves.

The basic parameters of our project are indicated in the dialogue below, a composite rendering inspired by approximately seven hundred conversations conducted over the course of one year of near-constant CD-playing and especially vocal backseat-driving. The song titles are listed below, and the points of emphasis are fleshed out in the dialogue. If you find yourself humming the tune as you read or, worse, *singing* these songs without even having the lyrics before you, consider yourself already beyond salvation.

The Playlist

INSTRUCTIONS: Locate a disc with children's music. Ideally, this would have a wide variety of songs, including Christmas tunes and contemporary offerings from artists like Raffi. Instruct the children to make mental notes. (Explain what mental notes are.) Advise them to absorb key points. (Explain what key points are.) Then discuss the material in a manner consistent with the exchanges below.

"It's Raining, It's Pouring"

ME. Boys, we just heard it was raining and pouring with an old guy snoring. What does this song seem to be about?

LUCAS. Well, they said that he bumped his head and couldn't get up in the morning. Um, Dad? Doesn't that mean he's *dead?* I mean, if he hit his head and then didn't ever wake up again, is he still alive?

ME. Let's not get ahead of ourselves.

WILLS. Wait, he's *dead?* Hah! A dead guy! That's so funny!

ME. Death isn't really funny, Wills. Let's start at the beginning. What's the scene?

LUCAS. It's raining and pouring.

ME. What does the weather add to the song?

LUCAS. I don't know.

ME. I don't know, either. Maybe they just said it was *pouring* so they could rhyme with *snoring.*

WILLS. What's *rain?*

ME. It's tears from the clouds. So, what else happens in this song?

LUCAS. Well, there was some rain, which maybe doesn't matter, and then the guy was snoring. But then he went to bed. Dad, why did he go to bed if he was already snoring? Doesn't that mean he was already asleep? How can you snore before you go to sleep? Was he asleep in some place that wasn't his bed? Is that why he was snoring before bed? I mean, before he died or whatever?

WILLS. Wait, I love s'mores! I want to go s'moring!

LUCAS. Not *s'mores*, Wills. Snores! You know, it's that loud noise adults make when they sleep. Like this [*making a helicopter sound*].

WILLS. Oh, yeah. Like the sound Dad makes?

ME. I don't make that sound! Why do you only hear things that aren't there? Come on, guys. What can we learn from this song?

LUCAS. Well, if it's raining and pouring, and you're an old man who is sleeping somewhere that's not your bed, be careful about going to bed, because you are probably going to bump your head and then die.

ME. Yeah, I guess, but . . . well, let's try the next song. You guys have heard this one many times.

"The Wheels on the Bus"

WILLS. That song is dumb.

LUCAS. That bus driver is grumpy. He just keeps telling everyone to move around. That's like you, Dad!

ME. I don't sound like that. By the way, move your booster seat over a bit.

WILLS. Whoa, *awesome*! That song is about our dad!

ME. No, it isn't! I'm not like that bus driver at all. Let's focus here—what is this song about?

LUCAS. I don't know. It's just a bus that goes around and around.

ME. I know, but where is it going?

LUCAS. I don't know. Do you?

ME. No, not really. Actually, I think this song only exists so that parents can do silly hand gestures with babies in swimming classes. I always felt like an idiot swinging your arms like windshield wipers.

WILLS. That song is dumb.

ME. Yeah, it is. Okay, let's go to the next one.

"Five Little Monkeys"

ME. Who is jumping on the bed?

BOTH. Monkeys!

ME. How are monkeys like little kids?

WILLS. They poop a lot! That's funny. Um, can we have some—wait, what are they called again?

ME. No. How else are they like little kids?

LUCAS. They eat bananas?

ME. Right. They also scratch themselves in inappropriate places. But what is the lesson here?

WILLS. Can I have a banana?

ME. No. What are you supposed to *learn* from this story about little monkeys?

WILLS. Don't be a monkey?

ME. Not exactly.

LUCAS. Don't jump on the bed?

ME. Right. Why?

WILLS. Because the doctor will yell at your mommy?

ME. Well, I guess. But why was the doctor yelling at the mommy?

LUCAS. Because she was letting all the monkeys jump on the bed even though they kept falling off?

ME. Right. Shouldn't she have figured out the monkeys were somewhat accident-prone?

LUCAS. Also, they should have been doing a more appropriate activity before bedtime.

WILLS. Can I have a banana? Or a monkey?

ME. No. So, it sounds like we agree that jumping on the bed is bad. We aren't going to do that, are we?

[*No response.*]

ME. Okay, moving on. This next song is about a little bunny.

"Little Bunny Foo Foo"

ME. Do you remember when your teachers explained bullying?

BOTH. Yeah.

ME. So, is Foo Foo a bully?

WILLS. Yeah. He's bad.

LUCAS. Well . . .

ME. Why the hesitation, Lucas?

LUCAS. I thought bullies were scary. How can you be a bully if you're a bunny and your name is Foo Foo?

ME. That's true.

LUCAS. Bunnies are soft, furry, and nice.

WILLS. You hate bunnies, Dad! You always shoot the hose at them!

ME. I don't *hate* bunnies. But yes, I do take issue with them eating stuff from my garden. Perhaps Foo Foo is not a normal sort of bully. But is he being bad?

LUCAS. Yes. He's hitting the field mice.

ME. And do they like it?

BOTH. No.

ME. Remember how we've talked about *consequences?* When you do something bad, there are consequences—like maybe going to bed early. What are Foo Foo's consequences?

LUCAS. He gets turned into a goon.

WILLS. What's a *goon?*

ME. I don't know. Does that matter?

LUCAS. Well, what if he *likes* being a goon? I mean, that isn't really a punishment, is it?

ME. Maybe not. Maybe he should have been turned into a field mouse so he could get hit on the head by a mean bunny.

LUCAS. Wasn't the Good Fairy actually kind of a bully for turning him into that? Why would the Good Fairy hurt another creature?

ME. I don't know. Ask Mom.

"Three Blind Mice"

ME. In the last song, we had a bunny who was hitting rodents, but what's happening in this one?

LUCAS. A lady is cutting the tails off mice?

ME. Right. Is that nice of her?

WILLS. What does *blind* mean?

ME. It means you can't see. Your eyes don't work right.

LUCAS. So, how do they run?

ME. Well, their legs work, but I guess they don't necessarily know where they're going.

LUCAS. So, what if they didn't *mean* to run after the farmer's wife? If they can't see, how did they chase her? Maybe they wanted to escape.

WILLS. Maybe she was made of cheese!

ME. Good point, Wills. Lucas, what if they weren't *blind* mice? Would that change the situation? And what about cutting off their tails? Now they don't have the use of their eyes or their tails. They're just three mice with stumps for butts, stumbling around in dark glasses.

WILLS. Dad said *butts*! Can I have some cheese?

LUCAS. What did she do with their tails?

ME. I have no idea. All right, this next one involves another injury. But we want to focus on what's called *problem-solving*, because these characters have some trouble doing that. Not trouble seeing the problem; just trouble doing anything about it. Or at least that's what I think. Actually, I'm not really sure what this song is about.

"There's a Hole in My Bucket"

WILLS. That song is dumb.

LUCAS. I don't get it. There's a hole in a bucket, and the boy just keeps asking how to fix it. Then the girl tells him how, but he always says it won't work. And then they talk about the hole again.

ME. Yup, that's it.

LUCAS. That song *is* dumb.

WILLS. Can I have a hole?

ME. No. Who wants to always skip that song? This next one we usually hear around Christmas, but it has a message that I want you guys to think about all year long.

"Santa Claus Is Coming to Town"

LUCAS. Oh, that reminds me! For Christmas, I want the LEGO 59 X Turbo Blaster—

ME. Wait a second, we aren't talking about lists for presents; we're talking about *Santa's* list. What does Santa write down in this song?

LUCAS. Kids who are naughty or nice?

ME. Right. What does *naughty* mean?

LUCAS. Acting like Wills?

WILLS. I want a football!

ME. Wills, what does *naughty* mean?

WILLS. I don't know.

ME. It means bad. Are you ever bad?

WILLS. No. Can I have a football? With some cheese?

ME. I'm not the one to ask. I'm not Santa Claus—but I do know that he keeps a list of who is being good and bad all year long. That means he's watching all the time. He sees everything you do. Remember when I told you guys about that thing called The Government? Santa is like The Government, but he has even more power because he can enter your house without a warrant.

LUCAS. Through the chimney?

ME. Exactly.

LUCAS. But Dad, we don't have a chimney.

ME. Exactly. Say, did you guys happen to hear that part about being good for the entire year? Seriously, Santa sees everything. And the elves can't make toys for naughty boys—and especially not footballs. Or cheese.

LUCAS. Dad, how do elves make LEGOs? In the movies, they only have hammers, nails, and wood. But LEGOs are made of plastic.

ME. I don't know. Magic, I guess. Our final song is also about Christmas. Think about Rudolph and how everyone treated him.

"Rudolph the Red-Nosed Reindeer"

ME. Have you guys been laughed at and called names?

BOTH. Yeah.

ME. By whom?

BOTH. Him [*pointing at each other*].

ME. Do you like it?

BOTH. No.

WILLS. What's a *reindeer*?

LUCAS. *Rudolph* is a reindeer, Wills! They fly Santa Claus around the world.

WILLS. I want a reindeer for Christmas! And a football made of cheese! And also, a reindeer. Wait, I mean—

ME. Why were the other reindeer mean to Rudolph?

LUCAS. Because he looked different?

ME. Right. And did that make Rudolph feel good?

LUCAS. No.

ME. Do you guys remember the video we watched last Christmas, the one with the talking snowman who tells the story of how Rudolph had the bright red nose? Remember how Rudolph's dad, Donner, tried to cover the red nose with a fake reindeer nose, because he was embarrassed by how his son looked?

BOTH. Yeah.

ME. Was that a good thing for a dad to do?

BOTH. No.

ME. I promise I'll never make you guys wear fake noses, but what did that do for the story? What was its significance? Why did everyone all of a sudden like Rudolph in the end?

LUCAS. Because he could *help* them?

ME. Right. First, they shunned him, banishing him to the Island of Misfit Toys, but once they found out they could use him for something—like, as a headlight—then they were nice to him. And so, what would you say is the moral of the story?

LUCAS. Have a red nose?

ME. No. Well, not entirely. The moral is, even if you're different, the normal people (or reindeer) will tolerate you if you can advance their interests in some way. If you can *do* something for them. You see? That's how you go down in history.

WILLS. That song is dumb.

DRIVING ME CRAZY

There are biological underpinnings that help explain why young children drive us crazy. Adults have a fully developed prefrontal cortex, the part of the brain that sits just behind the forehead, while the prefrontal cortexes of young children are barely developed at all. The prefrontal cortex controls executive function, which allows us to organize our thoughts and (as a result) our actions. Without this ability, we cannot focus our attention.

-Jennifer Senior

I AM NOT ASKING FOR MUCH. We have errands to run, and all I want the boys to do is put on their shoes. It would be nice if they would also clean up their rooms and brush their teeth, but I know better than to even hope for that. Those things only happen on television.

I give them a timeframe. I announce that we will be leaving in five minutes. And I place their shoes by the front door.

But it never works.

They just dawdle, conspiring to force our errands to another day. This usually takes the form of pretending not to hear me, while instead singing songs, poking each other, fighting, remembering things we would bring with us if we actually went somewhere, asking me where all those things are, spending another ten minutes trying to find those things around the house, and then losing every one of them as they wander the halls looking for their shoes.

After this goes on for a while, I manage to box them in, staking a position opposite the front door. Going *out* is their only option: there is no escape to the interior of the home. The two young humans that I must bring with me at ten o'clock on this Tuesday morning are sitting right in front of me. And their shoes are right in front of them.

All they need to do is put them on.

It seems so easy.

Just the shoes, boys.

Put on your damn shoes.

Please?

I could just do it myself, of course; and if I had, we would already be on our way. But since they are now ages five and eight, and thus essentially adults, it's time for them to do these things for themselves. After all those years of kneeling down to tie their shoes for them, as they busied themselves by patting me on the head or playing with my hair, I've tapped out. I taught them both how to perform this task, and now it's their responsibility.

And it's a simple charge, really: one that lab tests indicate even little monkeys can handle—little monkeys who, we must note, only need to be told once. For some reason, however, children—or maybe just my children, although I doubt it—cannot complete this and other basic assignments. It seems like they're not paying attention, which is often the case; but it's also true that, as the epigraph for this chapter indicates, the portion of a child's brain that handles executive function is not yet fully developed.

Certainly, there are some children better at this than others—yet when you say to your average kid, "Do this thing," they just look at you and mutter, "Okay," while then forgetting what it is they are supposed to do before they have even finished agreeing to do it. For such easily distractible creatures, rates of task completion can routinely hover around the level of chance.

That is, unless they *want* something. Or unless they want to go somewhere. Then, it's a whole different story. Then, children—or maybe just my children, although I doubt it—somehow find their brains supremely well developed and ready to take them on their way to whatever destination they have in mind. Then, all of a sudden, they are highly motivated to leave.

Impatient, even.

"Daaaaaaaaaaaaaaaaaaaaaad!" Wills bellows, as he does whenever he reaches this point and always with a five-year-old's familiar tone of insistence minus awareness.

"What, Wills?" I answer, even though I should know better.

"Can we *go* somewhere?" he asks. "It seems like we never go places anymore."

A better man might harness this desire to leave and find a way to turn it into a teachable moment, but all I can manage is snarky false enthusiasm.

"Oh, you would like to *go* somewhere?" I say. "What a great idea! Sure, we could go somewhere."

"Wait—*what*?! We're going somewhere?" he wonders, somehow sounding surprised—shocked, actually, as if he's just learned that Elmo is actually Grover.

"Yes," I concede in a cagey tone, hesitant as ever to invest much in this conversation.

"Where?" he wants to know. "Can we go to Chuck E. Cheese's?"

"No," I respond.

"Why not?" he demands, as if a five-year-old were ever in a position to make demands.

"No," I respond. Again.

I know this doesn't really answer his question, but as far as I am concerned, we don't need a reason not to go to Chuck E. Cheese's.

"But we *want* to go there," he adds, as if that were ever my concern.

"Oh, I'm sorry," I say in a completely insincere manner, like the customer-service representative on the other end of the line who doesn't give a crap about your broken microwave handle. "I didn't realize that you *want* to go there. That changes everything."

"Yay! We get to go to Chuck E. Cheese's!" he shouts, excited beyond belief.

"No!" I bark, realizing he's missed the sarcasm in my voice. "We are *not* going to Chuck E. Cheese's."

"But you *said* we were going there," he presses, because he hears what he wants to hear.

"Actually," I press back, "you asked if we could go there and I said *no*—just like I do every other time you ask."

"But you didn't say *no*," he keeps pressing.

"Yes, I *did*," I keep pressing back. "Check the transcript."

(I often say stuff like that because it's funny to see him walking around looking for a transcription machine that doesn't exist.)

"Besides," I add, "Chuck E. Cheese's doesn't even open until midnight. Now put on your shoes. We have places to go."

The shoes eventually get on, but not before a few more rounds of singing, poking, and fighting, after which the boys decide to dance the cha-cha, ask for lunch, declare they're not actually hungry, make a few more messes, and then head to their rooms to gather things to bring with us to Chuck E. Cheese's.

EVEN THOUGH HE IS SITTING only three feet away from me in the car, Wills acts as if we're having a conversation at the Indianapolis 500.

"When will we *be* there?!" he roars.

"Not for a while," I say. "We're still in the driveway."

"What?!" he snaps, sounding indignant. "What's taking us so long?"

I can tell from his voice that he's really had it with all this delay. First, we couldn't leave because of the impossible shoe assignment. Then there was that terrible rumor about canceling the trip to Chuck E. Cheese's that we never planned on taking in the first place. In first-world terms, this has been a rough morning.

"We will be there when we get there," I respond.

It's all I'm willing to say. The reader can probably understand why.

"But *when?*" he insists, unsatisfied with my politician's response. "In how many *minutes?*"

While he has now asked the question in terms of minutes, employing a real unit of time, it's still hard to take him seriously. The boy has no conception of time. A minute may as well be a light year. Or twelve.

"We'll be there in fifteen minutes," I say, even though it's pointless.

"In *fifteen* minutes?" he confirms, with an inflection indicating it's partly a restatement and partly a question.

I expect to hear my answer bouncing around his head a few times, making a *cling, clang, clank* sound as lights flash and puffs of smoke appear. But no. There is nothing. Just silence. I usually love the quiet, which I vaguely recall from my pre-child days, but this variety is all wrong. This is the quiet before the storm.

"But, um . . . how many *is* that, Dad?" he eventually asks, indicating the arrival of the storm.

The way he's saying this indicates he's perturbed, probably annoyed at having to continue posing simple questions to a simpleton father who's been misunderstanding him all morning long—and for several years before that. I'm accustomed to puzzling over mind-bending inquiries from this boy, especially doozies such as, "Dad, what color is blue?" and, more often than you would think, "I forget—what's the name of Earth again?" But the present line of questioning is all new, and I'm not exactly sure what to say.

"How many *is* that?" I reply, with an inflection indicating it's partly a restatement and partly a question. "Wills, are you asking me how many minutes is *fifteen* minutes?"

Now I *also* sound perturbed, annoyed at having to parry with a boy who doesn't listen to me, can't read a clock, and will soon ask for the same information again, because he will have forgotten he already asked for it. This isn't quite like talking to a wall; it's actually worse. The wall doesn't talk back to you.

I know I could just turn up the radio and ignore him, or draw the two of them into a distractive fraternal conflict by saying I can smell that someone in the backseat just farted.

But I don't.

Instead, I keep trying to figure out how to respond to this fabulous question from Wills that actually comes with its own built-in answer. He's my little boy, and I need to make sense of him. Somehow.

"Fifteen is fifteen," I offer, valiantly, after thinking about it for a bit. "That's how many it is, Wills. Fifteen."

I realize this response is redundant, but whatever. I'm tired.

"I know, but how many *is* that?" he tries once again. The inflection in his voice says he's thinking: *Why is my dad so dumb?*

"What do you mean, 'how many *is* that'?" I respond. The inflection in my voice says I'm thinking: *At least he's good at sports.*

Clearly, I need to figure out some way to make him stop talking—I mean, I need to figure out something to say so he'll feel satisfied in his understanding of this matter and so he'll revert to bothering his brother for a bit while I instead listen to people call in to sports-talk radio shows and propose trades that make absolutely no sense for any of the teams involved. It's been slow-going with Wills this morning, and I've given up any hope of lights or smoke; but with the right formulation, we might still have a shot at a *cling* or a *clank*.

"Okay, Wills," I say, digging deep into my bag of tricks. "Do you know what *one* minute is?"

The nod I can see in the rearview mirror suggests he does.

"Well," I continue, "fifteen minutes is like one minute—but with fourteen little friends."

I smile because it's funny to think of minutes having little friends.

"Oh!" he replies, suggesting an epiphany. "You mean it's like one minute . . . but then with fourteen other minutes?"

It seems we've finally located today's phrase that pays: a rendering to appease him even if he still doesn't totally get the concept. And so, as we drive along, it gets quiet for a few blissful minutes, allowing me to drift into thought, wondering: *Why are people who drive that kind of car always so annoying?* And then: *Wait, is that guy picking his nose?*

Which is a wonderful respite, considering all I've been through this morning, until my Spidey sense tingles. Trouble is coming. Soon.

"So . . . um . . . well . . . um . . . *Daddy?*"

I can already tell this is going to be dangerous. Perhaps catastrophic. If he had *immediately* come back at me with a "Daddy?" it would have been much better; it would have meant just a continuation of our conversation from its last exchange. But now he's been mulling things over, and I fear he's about to launch us in an unfortunate direction.

"*Yes*, Wills?" I say, as calmly as I can, practicing the deep-breathing techniques I've been working on since he was born.

"Um," he posits, giggling a bit because he's amused by the sound of my funny breathing, "is that . . . um . . . is fifteen minutes . . . um . . . is that like *five* minutes?"

This wasn't the kind of unfortunate direction I feared; this was an unfortunate direction I didn't even know existed. Now, not only were we not making much progress with our existential investigation of minutes, we weren't even holding ground on the basics of cardinal numbers.

"Wills," I try again, resigned to a lifetime of high blood pressure, "does *five* minutes make sense to you? You asked if fifteen minutes is like five minutes. Does that mean you understand five minutes?"

He gives me another nod in the rearview mirror.

"Okay, good. Then just take five minutes, add another five minutes, and then add *another* five minutes, and you'll have fifteen minutes. All right? Make sense?"

"*Oh!*" he squeals, bespeaking another epiphany, even though epiphanies are supposed to be rare events. It seems like now he *does* get it, but I'm still cautious. I know how this boy operates: how he tries to draw you into a trap before getting trapped himself because he was so excited to show you the trap that he ended up taking his own bait.

Sometimes I take advantage of this element of his personality, tying him up with riddles like, "What's the sound of one foot burping?" Or replying with only a non sequitur in the toy store, such as, "I'm sorry, bud, but roses are red, so we can't get that ball." And even throwing him serious thought problems, wondering, "How many zombies does it take to eat a million fruit snacks on Jupiter?" But when I'm not proactive enough to be proactive, he gets to me first. Which puts me on the defensive. Which isn't where I want to be.

"Daddy," he wonders, returning to the scene of the crime and again using that tone that tells me something bewildering is about to follow, "is that . . . so . . . um . . . is that like *six* minutes?"

What a delightful day this has been. As opposed to being deep in contemplation of proposed seven-way trades between teams that "Mikey from Jersey" barely sputtered out before the sports-talk radio hosts shot him down, I am instead deep in conversation about whether fifteen minutes is "like" five minutes—and then, for some reason, whether one or both of them is like six minutes.

Seriously, *six* minutes? At least five and fifteen are under the same umbrella of factors and multiples. But *six*? Where the hell did six minutes come from? We were now giving back all the gains for the day, as financial analysts say when the stock market tanks at 3:55 p.m. EST because someone broke the news that a powerful CEO was identified in a sex tape with a porpoise. Our shares were plummeting like a cinder block in the East River. We would soon have to liquidate. Wills was only a few steps away from asking whether fifteen minutes is like chicken broth. Or Chuck E. Cheese's.

YOU'RE NEVER GOING TO BELIEVE THIS, but because I was so distracted thinking about how Wills can never focus, I missed a turn. Isn't that ironic? I was so immersed in my explanation of when we might get there, that now I have no idea where we are. I know we are in the right zip code, or at least the right area code, yet I also know we are not presently where I had intended for us to be.

But do the boys know that?

This happens now and again, and usually the backseat drivers are unaware, busying themselves by fighting over the book or game that both of them want only because the other one wants it. Still, sometimes they sense the situation; sometimes they realize I'm looking around a bit more than usual and trying to pretend like I know where I'm going. They can occasionally be perceptive in these less-than-helpful sorts of ways.

"Daddy, are you *lost?*" Wills asks, after noticing me driving in circles.

I can tell from his tone that he now feels even more confident than usual—probably because he thinks he won our recent six-minutes-equals-fifteen-minutes standoff.

"No," I say—and, in a sense, that's true. I'm not really "lost"; I just don't know where we are at this exact moment. This is my version of the story, and, as a parent, I'm allowed to take some liberties with the truth. Don't forget how busy "Santa Claus" is every Christmas Eve.

"Daddy's lost!" Wills concludes, once again failing to listen to me.

Then, as he says this, I miss *another* turn and mutter a certain word I actually say quite a lot but usually try to keep from them. I thought I might have swallowed the end of this utterance, giving me some plausible deniability, but guess who heard me. Or thought he heard me.

"Wait, *what?*" Wills asks. "What did you say, Daddy?"

The young philosopher of time now sounds as excited as he did when he first heard we were going to Chuck E. Cheese's.

"I didn't say anything," I insist, this time rooting my prevarication in the spirit of both the Easter Bunny and the Tooth Fairy.

"Yes, you *did*," Wills asserts, gleeful at the thought of having something on me.

"Yeah, Dad," Lucas adds, cautiously, apparently willing to abet this act of patricide even though he would never lead the attack himself. "We heard you."

"No," I insist once again. "Actually, you *mis*heard me."

"Nuh-uh, Dad," they say in unison. "We heard it. You said—"

"What?" I demand to know, staring them down in the rearview mirror. "Tell me, guys. What is it that you think I said?"

This is terrible of me to do, since it takes them outside the limited protections of kid-form due process, but I don't care. They started it. Well, actually, I started it, but you know what I mean. They're the ones making something of it.

As they try to figure out their response, I can see they're torn. They know the rule about not saying bad words, but they aren't sure whether it applies to a situation where they're just repeating a word they *think* their father said. They want to know whether that counts as "saying" the word for purposes of getting in trouble, but I won't tell them. They want me to weigh in on their hypothetical question, but I refuse to pre-judge the case. They would like immunity from prosecution, but I won't grant it. The world is not a fair place.

I can hear them whispering through their options, goading each other to test the waters. The smart move, of course, would be to just let this slide, as I let things slide from time to time. But they aren't always known for choosing the smart move. And you can probably guess who comes forward to showcase the less-than-smart move they've chosen.

"Daddy," Wills begins. "We heard you. You said *sh—*"

"No, I *didn't*," I aver, denying the charge before he can even file it—just as the Great Pumpkin and the Elf on the Shelf would want me to.

A brief silence follows as we all consider our positions.

Then, at the next red light and for no particular reason, I hand them both heaping bowls of Goldfish crackers from the special bag of favors I keep on the floor of the passenger side of the car. In my experience as a father, there are some misunderstandings that only Goldfish can resolve.

I know what you're thinking, but, in a semi-technical sense, an action like this is "bribery" only if it involves a public official. We tend to misuse that term in everyday conversation. You can't bribe little kids when you're the boss of them. This was just a way for us all to get where we wanted to be.

Indeed, while the boys take a break from mishearing things, chomping away on a nutritious snack, I eventually get back onto some roads I recognize. And, for a while, everything seems okay . . . that is, until the Board of Censors forgets he was supposed to forget something.

"I'm *still* going to tell Mommy!" Wills eventually announces, as Goldfish swim out of his mouth.

He thinks he has me here, but he doesn't. At least not entirely. I'm not afraid of Mommy. Besides, what can he tell her? Does he think he can circumvent the bar on saying a bad word just by speaking it to Mommy? What is Mommy, some sort of disinterested observer? Is Mommy neutral, like Switzerland?

At the same time, why take a chance? Mommy gets frustrated with me enough as it is, and I don't need her getting a whiff of this. So, I double down on my initial approach, handing Lucas another heaping bowl of hush money while giving him a look in the rearview mirror that says: *Your birthday is coming up soon.*

Then I shift my glance to Wills and declare, with sadness in my voice, "Okay, little buddy, if that's what you want to do. I guess I'll just eat this piece of gum all by myself."

This is *also* terrible of me to do, but I need this problem to go away, and Wills fancies gum as much as I enjoy brown spirits with higher proofs.

We good now? my eyes ask, as some bubble gum makes its way to the backseat in a brown paper bag. To be clear, I'm not paying him to be quiet, because I've tried that before and it's objectively impossible. It's more that I'm counting on, and perhaps even prolonging, the underdevelopment of his prefrontal cortex—expecting and perhaps even encouraging him to forget to execute a task that really doesn't need to be executed at all. Especially now that we've arrived at Chuck E. Cheese's.

FATHERHOOD APTITUDE TEST

Like dogs or other house pets, new dads are filled with good intentions but lacking the judgment and fine motor skills to execute well.

-a Clorox commercial

IN THE SPACE BELOW, you will find a fatherhood aptitude test, an exercise designed to evaluate your instincts, assess your sensibilities, and determine what you have learned from this book. As you contemplate the hypothetical situations within these propositions, be honest. No one wins by cheating—except, of course, those who cheat, end up winning, don't get caught, and don't feel any remorse. Unfortunately, those people do win by cheating.

In essence, this test is like those television programs that devise vexing moral situations and then foist them upon unsuspecting passersby for the delight of the viewing audience. You know, like when a baker with a big white hat and chocolate sauce all over his crotch jumps out of a porta potty with a tray of pastries in his hands and then asks some poor pedestrian to help him deliver the goods to a local orphanage. He'd do it himself, he says to the stranger, but he's bound by a restraining order.

As the viewer, you are meant to play along—to consider whether you would make the orphan kids happier by delivering the pastries or whether you would walk away as quickly as possible from a man with a big white hat who just came out of a porta potty with chocolate sauce all over his crotch.

On the one hand, all kids love sugary treats; but on the other hand, those sweet delights just emerged from the kind of waste containment unit that sits at outdoor summer music festivals for days on end, capturing hazards so pungent they kill all the nearby grass.

INSTRUCTIONS: In the twenty items below you will find a basic proposition and supplemental explanation. Respond to each proposition by marking AGREE, DON'T KNOW, or DISAGREE.

1. A four-year-old is mature enough to play poker.

Not strip poker, for sure. Just normal five-card draw subsidized by funds from his piggy bank. If the boy chooses to play, he might increase his savings and eventually have enough for the motor scooter he has always wanted. But if he loses—perhaps because the game wasn't explained all that well to him—he might have to relinquish some of the allowance doled out earlier in the day. And maybe some of the allowance doled out on other days, too. Which could be a valuable lesson about gambling that he would never forget.

AGREE   DON'T KNOW   DISAGREE

2. When your child is fascinated by the idea of competitive vomiting, it's okay to count every dry-heave as its own distinct barf. As in the following sequence:

"Daddy, how many times have I thrown up?"
"Well, you threw up stuff, like food or water, only the first four times, but then you threw up no stuff for another twenty-eight times."
"Wow! So, how many throw-ups is that? Like nine?"
"No, it would be four plus twenty-eight. That's more than nine. If we're counting every time you made a loud sound like *blehhhhhhhhhhh*, then it's more like thirty-two."
"Awesome! Thirty-two barfs? Wait until I tell my friends!"

AGREE   DON'T KNOW   DISAGREE

3. Hiding from your children for the better part of the afternoon helps them develop problem-solving skills and a healthy sense of independence.

It's important that the kids are old enough to play in another room. You also need to be available to provide food, water, and medical assistance if absolutely necessary. Mostly, we are talking about keeping yourself out of sight, since seeing you will remind them of all the things they "need," even though they didn't need them at any point before. If there is quiet play going on, don't disturb it. Take the long way to get from one room to another. Go out the side door and in the bedroom window on the second floor if you must, but avoid being seen. Hide in the closet, the garage, the dryer—anywhere, actually.

AGREE   DON'T KNOW   DISAGREE

4. There are times when one needs to change the clocks so that "bedtime" comes a bit earlier.

Time is an arbitrary concept. As a society, we already do the clock-changing thing twice a year, so this question simply probes your willingness to have a child get even more healthful rest, as opposed to hewing to social conventions like sleeping only when it's dark outside. When it's barely five o'clock in the evening, but feels much later, go ahead and make it so. But remember to change the clocks back after the child goes to bed so he doesn't think it's okay to get up in the middle of the night. Getting up in the middle of the night is never okay.

AGREE   DON'T KNOW   DISAGREE

5. One diaper per day is sufficient for the average infant.

We all know the diaper lobby drums up hysteria to boost sales. They have most of the parenting world fooled into believing families must have a reservoir of diapers on hand, while the truth of the matter is that one average diaper can easily hold a day's worth of waste.

AGREE   DON'T KNOW   DISAGREE

6. Part of learning about baseball is getting buzzed by the pitcher, even if it's your own father who is the one playing that chin music.

Say you were pitching to a cocky three-year-old who managed to get a few cheap hits off of you. And say he was showing you up by taking his time admiring the Wiffle ball that sailed a total of four feet in front of him. With your next pitch, isn't it your job to send a "message"? Isn't it better to learn the unwritten rules of baseball from your father before you go out into the world and encounter a little wannabe Bob Gibson?

AGREE   DON'T KNOW   DISAGREE

7. Children's books need to be revised while you are reading them. This makes the book more interesting for both the child who is listening and the adult who is reading. As in the following example:

ORIGINAL   Sunny the Bunny started eating her carrots in front of Roger the Raccoon, but Roger was sad because Sunny would not share with him.

REVISED   Sunny the Bunny started eating her carrots in front of Roger the Raccoon, but Roger was sad because Sunny would not share with him. This is why a lightning bolt came down from the sky and scorched Sunny. After that, Roger was very happy, because cooked rabbit is delicious, especially with fresh carrots.

AGREE   DON'T KNOW   DISAGREE

8. When the kids want a bedtime story and you are too tired to come up with anything original, it's okay to borrow a couple concepts from the Grimm Brothers, with a dash or two of Lewis Carroll, and some barely obscured characters imported from Walt Disney. As in the following example:

ONCE UPON A TIME, there was a girl who lived in the forest with some fairies. One day, she met a guy in the woods who was, for some reason, singing. She thought that was cool, even though it isn't, so they became friends. But then a mean old lady got mad at the younger woman and sent some bad guys after her. Which is why a hungry wolf went over to a grandmother's house and ate all the croutons that the little children had been dropping along the road—just as a cat with a big smile ran into a white rabbit who was late for an appointment he didn't even have with Mousey Mick and Ducky Don. THE END.

AGREE   DON'T KNOW   DISAGREE

9. During "sleep training," when it's unclear which party is being trained, the cool and rational parent in the home may need to secretly insert plugs into the ears of the parent who is not so cool and rational—also known as the parent who thinks she needs to rush into the room at the slightest sound of agitation from the terrorizing party.

We don't want to generalize here, but when one parent (the one who wants the baby monitor turned up so loud it can be heard in another state) comforts the baby every time he makes a noise, the little person obviously associates making noise with the return of the hugger and kisser. Thank you, Ivan Pavlov.

AGREE   DON'T KNOW   DISAGREE

10. When a kid is taking his nightly bath and he's been especially difficult that day, it's okay to quietly add a few ice cubes to the tub while he's distracted by shampoo in his eyes.

This should be self-explanatory.

AGREE   DON'T KNOW   DISAGREE

11. When you take kids to the grocery store, it's okay to make most purchasing decisions based solely on the answer to this question: "Would you eat this without whining?"

If the answer is "No," put the item back and conserve your energy. If the answer is "Yes," proceed through the following: "Are you *sure*? Even though it has these little things on it? Remember how you usually don't like little things?" Amount of nutrition, ease of opening, danger-ous preservatives, and even cost should all come into play only after it has been determined the kids will eat the food without complaint.

AGREE   DON'T KNOW   DISAGREE

12. He might be crying because he's happy.

This should also be self-explanatory.

AGREE   DON'T KNOW   DISAGREE

13. The general rule for Halloween is that an adult taking a child trick-or-treating is required to "check" the bag periodically, making it a bit lighter each time, while then apportioning the stash in a fair way at the end of the night. Or in a way that the adult thinks might be fair. In a way.

A child is young and in need of vitamins and other things that aren't in candy. He should get to keep some of the proceeds, but it's also important to make his bag more comfortable for him while he walks along. So, too, is it a good idea to establish a policy from an early age of taking one-fourth of the yield for the house, one-fourth for the adult security detail, and one-fourth for "incidentals," whatever those are.

AGREE   DON'T KNOW   DISAGREE

14. Batman is not a "superhero."

Batman suffered terrible childhood trauma, is really pissed off, works the right side of the law (mostly), and helps the residents of Gotham, but he's still just a guy with a utility belt. He's great in many ways, but there's nothing "super" about him. Kids heading onto the playground of life need the facts, and a good father needs to share his version of those facts. Even if that means reclassifying comic book characters.

AGREE   DON'T KNOW   DISAGREE

15. In order for your child to feel accepted in today's society, it's okay to pretend he has food allergies.

It does seem odd having to invent a disability just to be normal, but if you don't do this, your little one will be susceptible to torment from allergy bullies who will tease him about his ability to drink a glass of cow's milk, eat a PB & J with real peanut butter, or ingest gluten and other things no one heard of until everyone began worrying about them. Now is not the time to be asking epidemiological questions about whether we're making things worse by segregating kids from perceived threats; now is the time to fall in line and come up with an easy-to-endure allergy your child can call his own. A thing to avoid that won't be too challenging. Like squid. Or cumin.

AGREE   DON'T KNOW   DISAGREE

16. Whenever you fall victim to the Law of Simultaneous Compromise (LSC), it's time to start drinking.

The LSC recognizes that if two young children are present, two young children will end up simultaneously compromised to the extent that neither can be effectively managed, because both will create conditions to steal attention from the other. You can see the LSC at work when you're changing the diaper of a youngster who has destroyed his third onesie of the morning with an eruption that basically laughed at its containment plan as it blasted through eleven layers of polyurethane—while, at the same time, an older child emerges from the bathroom with a baby wipe hanging from his rear end, announcing, "Look, I have a tail!" Both parties are armed and extremely disgusting, and both call for immediate action because of the potential for fecal apocalypse, but neither situation can command your full attention due to the potential for devastation presented by the other.

AGREE   DON'T KNOW   DISAGREE

17. It's okay to be proud of your older son who has figured out how to snooker his little brother out of just about anything. We aren't saying entirely proud, because you need to be look-

ing out for the little one as well. However, it is charming to witness "trade" negotiations where an eight-year-old talks up the value of a piece-of-crap toy he never really liked just to make it *seem* more appealing as a commodity in an effort to acquire the new toy his little brother just got but doesn't really know how to use. What is even more impressive, is the tactic where the older one prematurely closes down talks, saying he just wants to go to his room and play with his robot with only one leg and no head—making it *seem* as if the broken device is so fun that he literally can't even discuss a trade anymore . . . only to be followed into that room by the naïve younger brother who would never survive in the wild.

AGREE   DON'T KNOW   DISAGREE

18. If there was no report, there was no crime.

When you're listening to a radio program and the hosts are interviewing some has-been athlete who blew it on a bonehead play in the championship game in 1979, breaking the hearts of long-suffering fans in some cold city in the Midwest, and you hear the sounds of a potential brawl downstairs, you just need to ignore the children. Yes, you can still hear one of them yelling "Daaaaaaaaaaaad!"—which is often followed by the other one whispering "pssssssss, pssssssss, pssssssss." As a courtesy, you might ask, "Is everything okay?" But this is mostly just to encourage kid-level problem-solving, probably involving more "pssssssss"-type sounds, followed by some combination of "you" and "don't" and "tell" and "me" and "I" and "won't." You know *something* occurred, but you neither investigated the matter nor got an official complaint. Which effectively means nothing happened.

AGREE   DON'T KNOW   DISAGREE

19. Young children with stillness issues require extensive blanketing at bedtime.

A boy who is very tired, but who will not remain still enough to fall asleep, may need to be saved from himself. This heroic effort involves bundling the little rascal with a base blanket to immobilize his torso—before wrapping a second layer to discourage leg movement, a third layer for the arms, and then a fourth layer to render the boy a cocoon. In thirty seconds, he will be asleep, and layers four and three can be removed; although, it doesn't hurt to leave layers two and one intact, just in case he stirs a bit.

AGREE   DON'T KNOW   DISAGREE

20. Mind games are perfectly acceptable devices in the pursuit of discipline.

One effective means of controlling little people (and big people) is to get into their heads with the idea that you *might* be watching. Consider the philosopher Jeremy Bentham's concept of a prison built around centralized observation, where the cells are visible at any given moment but where inmates cannot know whether they are being watched. Applying this notion to the management of young children, a father might make it seem like he's allowing a boy to play outside without supervision, while secretly keeping tabs on him from the window and waiting for even the slightest infraction. After witnessing a misstep or two, the father then states, "You know, I saw you throw that popsicle stick into the garden. Why do you hate the earth?" This creates an energy, even paranoia, in the lad who now thinks that his dad really *does* know everything—and definitely sees everything. Always a good thing.

AGREE   DON'T KNOW   DISAGREE

SCORING: Give yourself one point for every AGREE, zero points for a DON'T KNOW, and subtract one point for every DISAGREE. Then add up your score. A total of *twenty* indicates success. You are, or you could be, a great father. Anything less than that signifies failure. Try reading the book again.

CONCLUSION

When I was a boy of fourteen, my father was so ignorant I
could hardly stand to have the old man around. But when I
got to be twenty-one, I was astounded at how much the old
man had learned in seven years.

-Mark Twain

D EAR LUCAS AND WILLS,

The end has come. Not the end of days (to my knowledge), just
the end of this book. More traditional memoirs can wrap up their
accounts by reflecting on a year spent eating, praying, and loving, for
example; but a book like this, about a situation still in progress, finds
closure in a turning point. This turning point came when you were
both old enough for school and when our family was no longer stumbling through the earliest years of life with children.

The start of school represents the end of a certain phase of childhood and, just as much, a certain phase of parenthood. I want the final
chapter of this book to mark the completion of those phases, but I also
want to use this space to explain why I wrote this work in the first
place. Certainly, I could have written a preface or prologue to justify
the project; but, like any true rationalization, I felt a proper defense
should *follow* the offending actions, not precede them. I wanted you
guys to read my reflections on watching you grow up (so far), and
watching myself grow up with you, before sharing with you my reasons
for putting these thoughts in the form of a book.

You see, when I die, you won't be inheriting any fortune. And you
won't find my name emblazoned on any buildings. I will have worked
hard every day, will have played by the rules, and will have given it my
all in this life. But—and this is the point—all I will leave behind is you
guys. *You* are my legacy. And you are also why I'm here. I see that now.

As you know, this book began as a mess of notes I scribbled down during the three months of family leave that I took in 2005 and 2008. I was a different person back then, when I first became a father, and, in my mind, that's one of the most interesting things about parenthood: children can't ever really know what their parents were like *before* they became parents, can't truly understand the transformative effects of the experience, and can't necessarily apprehend, as was the case with me, how a guy could go from being no one's idea of a father to a man who now enjoys being called Dad.

When I took that first family leave, I could tell the experience was reshaping me, and I felt there was definitely a compelling story to tell about fatherhood in a changing world. But beyond jotting down thoughts, I couldn't do much to make this book a reality—couldn't dedicate time to a project of this sort. There were too many papers to grade, too many students to meet with, and too much scholarly writing I was supposed to be doing instead.

Still, as the years went along, and as I was the one doing most of the parenting in our household, I continued making notes whenever I could and believed it was important to somehow offer my perspective on the broader—and growing—phenomenon of fathers playing the sort of role that I do in the home.

The prospects for this book improved in 2012. Mom and I opted for a major life change, deciding to move to the Pacific Northwest, where we had gone to college and where Mom grew up. We both wanted a change of scenery and found that the longer we stayed on the East Coast, where we had been since starting graduate school, the more difficult it would be to uproot and achieve the better lifestyle we desired. And we also knew if we didn't go soon, we wouldn't go at all.

So, we made it happen.

When we moved in 2013, you guys were in third grade and kindergarten, respectively. Mom secured a job that would make our transition possible, and we both resigned the positions we had worked hard to attain. You were a mixture of sad and excited: sad that you were leaving behind friends but excited to be closer to family. It took some time, but you adjusted. And you now view our new city as your hometown.

In some ways, what we did was a bad lesson to teach—walking away from jobs we were fortunate to have. But in other ways, it was a good lesson for you, because the wellbeing of the family should come first. And when the chance for something great comes along, you need to take it. Or at least take a good, long look at it. Even if that chance presents an enormous challenge.

Which it has, perhaps most of all for me. All of a sudden, after teaching college classes for fifteen years, I was no longer a professor. You don't take tenure with you when you leave an institution, and there were really no comparable positions for me after we moved. Thus, I needed to find something new—needed to start all over again.

I struggled with this transition; and I still struggle with it, actually, having given up an identity of which I was so proud. Even so, life is now much better for us. We are where we want to be, we have a more sustainable arrangement, we enjoy a better balance of work and life, and I have come to appreciate how the decision to make this move mirrors the very growth and opportunity portrayed in the pages above. Like other things in my life, I didn't see this coming—and yet, here I am having finished this book.

When I began working on it full time in spring 2014, I knew the project would be a challenge, mostly because people kept telling me that books about "family" issues are only written by women, that women are the only ones who buy memoirs, that women don't like a "male" sense of humor, and so on. But I decided to write it anyhow.

As a man who is the "primary caregiver" (even though that term still sounds funny to me), I felt I could shine a new light on a familiar sight with carefully integrated essays showcasing characters, situations, and concerns recognizable to anyone who has, or once had, young children.

Which is where you guys come in. You have been both my inspiration and my data points. Right now, you think it's cool that your dad wrote a book "about" you, but you won't think that in a few years. Given that, I figured it was best to stick to a time when you were both young and sweet. And when I was neither of those.

As you read or re-read this book, you will enjoy learning or revisiting some things about your early years. And I think you will also appreciate learning or revisiting some things about me. I hope you feel the emotion within these pages: the struggles, the pain, the frustration, the apprehension, the confusion, and the angst—but also the aspiration, the awakening, the satisfaction, and the happiness I have realized as your father.

ONCE YOU GUYS HAVE KIDS, or get to the age where you consider starting a family, I hope you'll be willing to embrace new opportunities, just as I took advantage of options not generally available to men of my own father's era. There are some chances you take that can mean everything. I wouldn't be here if I hadn't taken a few of them. And in a certain sense, neither would you.

It's important to me that you see *this* as the moral of our story, the story you guys helped me write. Small steps, even uncomfortable ones, can take you far. They can guide you places you didn't even know you wanted to be. Take, or at least consider taking, some of those steps every day. Open yourself to the unknown. Be willing to fail. And don't ever let convention confine you.

Mom and I have tried to raise you well, but you will err, as all people do. You will do wrong, you will be wrong, and you will act less than yourself on bad days. It happens.

Yet you will also shine on good days. Please try to have more of those good days, and remember that there's always a way to make things better—to make yourself better and to improve everything and everyone around you. The world needs as much of that as possible.

You have heard me talk about this stuff before, usually after I lose my temper or set some other bad example for you. I have many flaws and many of those days where I act less than myself. But when I slip, I recover. And then I try harder. Which is all that I expect of you: that you recover, that you try harder, and that you always look to be better.

Finally, I want you to know that, as much as I love being your dad, it brings me even more joy to imagine you guys in this role. You aren't thinking about that right now (just as I didn't), and you may grow up never yearning for it (just as I didn't), but you never really know what's going to happen (just as I didn't).

If you do become a father, pull this book off the shelf and think about what I've written. Being a dad is hard, especially if you're trying to do it right. But you'll love it. You won't always love it, but you will ultimately love it. And you won't be good at it right away, but that's okay. Keep at it. No matter where you start, you can always become the "World's Best Dad." Really, you can. Both of you. Trust me. I've seen it happen.

Love,
Dad

ACKNOWLEDGMENTS

For their love and support, I would like to thank my parents, Bill and Jan Pinaire. When Lucas was born, they uprooted from the Midwest and moved to the East Coast. We could not have made it through that challenging time without the assistance of highly involved grandparents. When we decided to move to the Pacific Northwest, they came our way again and continue to play a vital role in our lives.

I would also like to thank Emily's parents, Bill and Nancy Baird. From the West Coast, they made regular trips east to see our boys, and their longer visits helped us manage young children and two careers. They, too, continue to play a vital role in our lives.

My gratitude goes, as well, to the friends and colleagues who read portions of this book while I was working on it and who offered valuable feedback along the way. This was an unconventional work from the start, and it's been a challenge finding the right way to present this kind of story to the world. I'm still not sure I found that right way, but the suggestions made for a better product at every turn.

For her unwavering faith and completely unrealistic aspirations for this book in its final form, I wish to thank my wife, Emily. She is an amazing person, a wonderful spouse, and a doting mother who inspires me every day.

And, finally, none of this would have been possible without the constant material, motivation, and companionship provided by my two sons, Lucas and Wills. I love them in a way I never could have predicted and never would have believed. They truly are the world's best kids—and that's not even hyperbole.

NOTES

page 1   **Epigraph.** John Lewis-Stempel, ed., *Fatherhood: An Anthology* (Woodstock: The Overlook Press, 2003), 36.

page 7   **Generation X dads.** See, e.g., National Center for Fathering, "Survey of Fathers' Involvement in Children's Learning," accessed July 2, 2016, http://www.fathers.com/documents/research/2009_Education_Survey_Summary.pdf; Kim Parker and Wendy Wang, "Modern Parenthood," March 14, 2013, http://www.pewsocialtrends.org/2013/03/14/modern-parenthood-roles-of-moms-and-dads-converge-as-they-balance-work-and-family/; Jo Jones and William Mosher, "Father's Involvement With Their Children: United States, 2006-2010," *National Health Statistics Reports* 71 (December 20, 2013).

page 12   **Epigraph.** Joint Resolution, Pub. L. No. 92-278 (1972).

page 21   **Fathers fail every day.** Michael Chabon, *Manhood for Amateurs* (New York: HarperCollins, 2009), 7.

page 23   **Epigraph.** U.S. Department of Defense, "DoD News Briefing—Secretary Rumsfeld and General Myers," February 12, 2002, http://archive.defense.gov/Transcripts/Transcript.aspx?TranscriptID=2636.

page 31   **Delivery rooms.** See Judith Walzer Leavitt, *Make Room for Daddy* (Chapel Hill: University of North Carolina Press, 2010), passim.

page 33   **Epigraph.** Robert Burns, "To a Mouse, on Turning Her Up in Her Nest with the Plough," accessed July 12, 2016, http://www.robertburns.org.uk/Assets/Poems_Songs/toamouse.htm.

page 42   **Epigraph.** Sheryl Sandberg, *Lean In: Women, Work, and the Will to Lead* (New York: Alfred Knopf, 2013), 108.

page 53   **Epigraph.** Lee T. Gettler, et al., "Longitudinal Evidence that Fatherhood Decreases Testosterone in Human Males," *Proceedings of the National Academy of Sciences* 108, no. 39 (September 2011): 16196.

page 53   **Manopause.** See Marissa Stephenson, "The Truth About 'Manopause,'" accessed July 30, 2016, http://www.mensjournal.com/health-fitness/health/the-truth-about-manopause-20140731. (Discussing David Von Drehle, "Manopause," *Time*, July 31, 2014.)

page 54   **Diminished testicles.** See Paul Raeburn, *Do Fathers Matter?* (New York: Scientific American/Farrar, Straus and Giroux, 2014), 75.

page 54   **Increased body mass index.** See "Fat Dads," *Oregonian*, August 12, 2015.

page 54   **Reduced IQ.** See Gary Greenberg and Jeannie Hayden, *Be Prepared* (New York: Simon & Schuster, 2004), 73.

page 58   **Benefits of a BabyBjörn.** See Pamela Paul, *Parenting, Inc.* (New York: Times Books, 2008), 37.

page 61   **Fathercraft.** Adapted with apologies. See Matthew Crawford, *Shop Class as Soulcraft* (New York: Penguin Books, 2010).

page 65   **Epigraph.** Sarah Schoppe-Sullivan, "Maternal Gatekeeping, Coparenting Quality, and Fathering Behavior in Families with Infants," *Journal of Family Psychology* 22, no. 3 (2008): 389–90.

page 65   **Tiger moms.** See Amy Chua, *Battle Hymn of the Tiger Mother* (New York: Penguin Books, 2011), passim.

page 67   **Titi monkeys.** See Raeburn, *Do Fathers Matter?*, 19.

page 73   **Safeway.** See Safeway Corporation, "Our Story," accessed January 30, 2015, http://www.safeway.com/ShopStores/Our-Story.page.

page 73   **Mom to Mom.** Safeway Corporation, "About Mom to Mom," accessed January 30, 2015, http://www.safeway.com/ShopStores/MMMomToMom-About.page.

page 79   **Epigraph.** Lewis-Stempel, ed., *Fatherhood*, 45.

page 97   **Proximate alternatives.** See, e.g., Daniel Kahneman, *Thinking Fast and Slow* (New York: Farrar, Straus and Giroux, 2011), passim.

page 105   **Epigraph.** Gerald J. S. Wilde, "Risk Homeostasis Theory: An Overview," *Injury Prevention* 4 (1998): 89–90.

page 117   **Epigraph.** Stephen Pinker, *The Stuff of Thought: Language as a Window into Human Nature* (New York: Penguin Books, 2007), 425.

page 117   **Commonly used letters.** See Pavel Mička, "Letter Frequency," accessed December 1, 2015, http://en.algoritmy.net/article/40379/Letter-frequency-English.

page 146   **Teletubbies.** See "Gay Tinky Winky Bad for Children," accessed November 15, 2015, http://news.bbc.co.uk/2/hi/276677.stm.

page 148   **Epigraph.** Louann Brizendine, *The Male Brain* (New York: Three Rivers Press, 2010), 88.

page 148   **Styles of caregiving.** See David Popenoe, "Life Without Father," Cynthia Daniels, ed., *Lost Fathers* (New York: Palgrave Macmillan, 2000), 39–40.

page 149   **Activation-exploration themes.** Kyle Pruett, *Fatherneed* (New York: Broadway Books, 2000), 28.

page 149   **Brain-cell connections.** See Lawrence Cohen, *Playful Parenting* (New York: Ballantine Books, 2001), 33 and Anthony DeBenedet and Lawrence Cohen, *The Art of Roughhousing* (Philadelphia: Quirk Books, 2010), 14.

page 155   **Boys vs. girls.** See Brizendine, *The Male Brain*, 21.

page 165   **Checklist.** See Atul Gawande, "The Checklist," *The New Yorker*, December 10, 2007.

page 172   **Epigraph.** Homer, *The Odyssey*, Book XII.

page 172   **Manuel Noriega.** See Roberto Suro, "After Noriega," *New York Times*, December 30, 1989.

page 172   **Barney as torture.** See BBC News, "Sesame Street Breaks Iraqi POWs," accessed May 20, 2015, http://news.bbc.co.uk/2/hi/middle_east/3042907.stm.

page 182   **Epigraph.** Jennifer Senior, *All Joy and No Fun* (New York: HarperCollins, 2014), 26.

page 193   **Epigraph.** Raeburn, *Do Fathers Matter?*, 12.

page 204   **Epigraph.** Attributed to Mark Twain, *Reader's Digest*, September 1937.

CPSIA information can be obtained
at www.ICGtesting.com
Printed in the USA
LVOW13s2313220518

578181LV00009B/263/P